WAR OF THE WORLDVIEWS

Other books by Gary DeMar

God and Government:
A Biblical and Historical Study

God and Government:
Issues in Biblical Perspective

God and Government:
The Restoration of the Republic

Ruler of the Nations:
Biblical Blueprints for Government

The Reduction of Christianity:
A Biblical Response to Dave Hunt
(with Peter J. Leithart)

Something Greater Is Here

Surviving College Successfully: A Complete
Manual for the Rigors of Academic Combat

The Debate over Christian Reconstruction

You've Heard it Said: 15 Biblical Misconceptions
that Render Christians Powerless

America's Christian History:
The Untold Story

Last Days Madness:
Obsession of the Modern Church

Study Smart:
A Guide to Academic Excellence

WAR OF THE WORLDVIEWS

Gary DeMar
Illustrations by Daniel Riedel

American Vision, Inc.
Atlanta, Georgia

©1994 by American Vision, Atlanta, Georgia.
All rights reserved. First edition.

No part of this publication may be reproduced, stored in a retrieval system, or transmitted in any form by any means, electronic, mechanical, photocopy, recording, or otherwise, without the prior, written permission of the publisher, except for brief quotations in critical reviews or articles.

Unless otherwise noted, all Scripture quotations are from the *New American Standard Version* of the Bible, copyrighted 1960, 1962, 1963, 1968, 1971, 1972, 1973, 1975.

Illustrations by Daniel Riedel.
Cover illustration and design by James Talmage.

War of the Worldviews was first published as the first seven chapters of *Surviving College Successfully*. The Preface and Introduction are new.

Published by American Vision, Inc.
10 Perimeter Way, B-175
Atlanta, Georgia 30339

Printed in the United States of America.

ISBN 0-915815-12-5

CONTENTS

Acknowledgments /*vii*
Preface /*ix*
Introduction /*1*

1. Preparing for Battle /*5*
2. Worldviews in Conflict /*27*
3. The Christian Worldview /*45*
4. Shopping for a God /*65*
5. Leaping into the Void /*81*
6. Spiritual Counterfeits /*103*
7. The Occult Explosion /*115*
8. Living in a Postmodern World /*131*
Conclusion /*145*

End Notes /*151*
Name Index /*165*
Subject Index /*167*
Scripture Index /*173*

ACKNOWLEDGMENTS

The first seven chapters of *The War of the Worldviews* appeared in a slightly different form as the first seven chapters of *Surviving College Successfully*, first published in 1988. In order to make this material available to a broader audience I thought it would be profitable to separate the chapters dealing with worldview issues from the study skills section of the earlier work. A new Introduction has been added as well as a Foreword and Conclusion. "Living in a Postmodern World" has been added as the eighth chapter.

Dr. Greg L. Bahnsen made invaluable suggestions to the first five chapters. His clear thinking, unequaled grasp of philosophical systems and traditions, and precision of language greatly enhanced the usefulness and clarity of these chapters. I would like to thank Marty Fields who wrote a substantial portion of "Living in a Postmodern World" for his work on this project. Much of the editorial credit for the new material belongs to my research assistant Jane McCallum.

PREFACE

On the evening of October 30, 1938, America went to war with Mars. Those who turned on their radios that evening heard a program of dance music interrupted by a series of startling news bulletins. On that Halloween evening, as they listened to the music of Ramon Raquello and his orchestra playing at the Meridian Room in the Hotel Park Plaza in downtown New York, unsuspecting radio listeners heard this message:

> Ladies and gentlemen, we interrupt our program of dance music to bring you a special bulletin from the Intercontinental Radio News. At twenty minutes before eight, central time, professor Farrell of the Mount Jennings observatory, Chicago, Illinois, reports observing several explosions of incandescent gas, occurring at regular intervals on the Planet Mars.[1]

News followed that a "huge, flaming object" had fallen to Earth on a farm in the neighborhood of Grovers Mill, New Jersey. A horrified radio audience listened as the army which had been sent to the scene was apparently obliterated by an unidentified force. More landings were soon reported in other parts of the country. Many in the stunned radio audience came to the frightening conclusion that Earth was the target of a full-scale invasion from the Planet Mars!

It was soon learned that the broadcast had been engineered by Orson Welles and the cast of *The Mercury Theater of the Air*. "The program offered fake news reports of a Martian invasion, which a surprisingly large segment of the population took to be the truth, causing widespread panic."[2] The broadcast was so convincing and the panic so great that the "Federal Communications Commission discussed taking disciplinary action, and lawyers for some people who had believed the broadcast threatened to prosecute the Mercury."[3]

WAR OF THE WORLDVIEWS

THE REAL WAR OF THE WORLDS

H. G. Wells's fictional *War of the Worlds*, which was the basis for Orson Welles's radio program, depicts a clash between very alien societies—one planetary world hell-bent on destroying another. The Martian attack was relentless. Cobra-like periscopes emitted pulverizing beams of energy that ravaged the countryside. The sleek and deceptively beautiful Martian flying machines destroyed everything in their path.

A similar war rages in our own day, although the invasion is not extraterrestrial in the usual sense. An alien worldview has made its way to planet Earth causing even greater devastation than the havoc depicted in the imaginative *War of the Worlds*. Today's real-life battle is between the worldview of biblical Christianity, where the infinite and sovereign God of the universe reigns and rules, and the worldview of man-centered philosophy, where finite and rebellious creatures work to rule and reign independent of God.

We will see no significant positive change in our culture until Christians first realize that we are in a war over ideologies that have personal, institutional, and societal implications. The confrontational language used by both sides of the worldview clash is no mere "literary device but an apt tool to describe the way in which the many issues contested in American public culture are being settled. . . . Both sides of the new cultural divide could agree with the editor of Publisher's Weekly who declared that the controversy over the arts and publishing was a 'war'—'a war that must be won.' "[4]

Many Christian leaders try to avoid conflict with secular ideologies by teaching that God's Word has little to say about issues beyond an individual's personal religious experience. They argue that ideological wars raging, for example, in the economic and political arenas should be of little concern to Christians since "our citizenship is in heaven" (Philippians 3:20).[5] Such a position assumes that the biblical message of the kingdom is exclusively internal, personal, and heavenly. Christians who hold this position can live with a disintegrating culture because they believe in the inevitability of societal decline. Consider these examples:

> • This world is not going to get any easier to live in. Almost unbelievably hard times lie ahead. Indeed, Jesus said that these coming days will be uniquely terrible. Nothing in all the previous history of the world can compare with what lies in store for mankind.[6]

PREFACE

- What a way to live! With optimism, with anticipation, with excitement. We should be living like persons who don't expect to be around much longer.[7]

- I don't like clichés but I've heard it said, "God didn't send me to clean the fish bowl, he sent me to fish." In a way there's a truth in that.[8]

Ted Peters concludes that these beliefs about present and future world conditions function "to justify social irresponsibility" that serves to comfort Christians "in their lethargy."[9]

KINGDOMS IN CONFLICT

While many Christians acknowledge the reality of an ideological and spiritual war, they conclude that there is nothing that can or should be done to fight it. "God's kingdom is not of this world," we are told (John 18:36). While Jesus states that His kingdom is not of this world, He nowhere states that His kingdom is not in and over this world. When Jesus said that His kingdom is not "of" this world, he meant that it does not derive its authority and power from the world.[10]

Christ's statement about His kingdom was made in response to Pilate's question about kingship and kingdoms. Even Pilate, an earthly ruler in Rome, understood the issue. Jesus' answer was framed in terms of Pilate's perspective. Would Jesus bring an army? How large would it be? Since He was said to be "King of the Jews" (Luke 23:3), would Jesus incite a rebellion among the Jews to usurp Pilate's authority? What weapons would He use? Pilate believed, as did many Jews of that day, that armed conflict alone could extend a kingdom. It was a king's duty to use the power of the military against an enemy. Since Jesus was a king, Pilate assumed He must command His army in the same way. This was the Roman way.

God's kingdom operates differently. There is no need for military armaments. The kingdom's power comes from above and works on the heart of man: "I will give you a new heart and put a new spirit within you; and I will remove the heart of stone from your flesh and give you a heart of flesh. And I will put My Spirit within you and cause you to walk in My statutes, and you will be careful to observe My ordinances" (Ezekiel 36:26-27). God wages His battle against the kingdoms of this world through the awesome power inherent in His Word, energized by His

Spirit: "For though we walk in the flesh, we do not war according to the flesh, for the weapons of our warfare are not of the flesh, but divinely powerful for the destruction of fortresses" (2 Corinthians 10:3-4). It's the power of *regeneration*, not revolution, that brings about change to individuals who then reform families, churches, businesses, and every other feature of God's kingdom.

Christians are to destroy "speculations and every lofty thing raised up against the knowledge of God." We are to take "every thought captive to the obedience of Christ" (2 Corinthians 10:5). This is kingdom living in the power of God's Spirit. The kingdoms of this world are at war with the kingdom of Jesus Christ, and it is the duty of all Christians to be involved in that war until the gates of Hades no longer stand (Matthew 16:18). Those who desire to obliterate the Christian worldview will not relax their assault. Escape from the field of battle is treason.

NO COMPROMISE

A. A. Hodge, Professor of Systematic Theology at Princeton Seminary in the latter part of the nineteenth century, made the case that the kingdom of God on earth is without borders, "but aims at absolute universality, and extends its supreme reign over every department of human life."[11] The implications of such a view are obvious: "It follows that it is the duty of every loyal subject to endeavour to bring all human society, social and political, as well as ecclesiastical, into obedience to its law of righteousness."[12] Hodge believed that there are comprehensive societal ramifications to the preaching and application of the gospel.

> It is our duty, as far as lies in our power, immediately to organize human society and all its institutions and organs upon a distinctively Christian basis. Indifference or impartiality here between the law of the kingdom and the law of the world, or of its prince, the devil, is utter treason to the King of Righteousness. The Bible, the great statute-book of the kingdom, explicitly lays down principles which, when candidly applied, will regulate the action of every human being in all relations. There can be no compromise. The King said, with regard to all descriptions of moral agents in all spheres of activity, "He that is not with me is against me." If the national life in general is organized upon non-Christian principles, the churches which are embraced within the universal assimilating power of that nation will not long be able to preserve their integrity.[13]

PREFACE

Compromise is impossible. Conflict is inevitable. Neutrality is inconceivable. Spiritual and ideological wars will continue whether Christians want to believe it or not. The question is, Are Christians prepared to fight?

NOT WITHOUT WEAPONS

God has not left Christians defenseless against the antagonistic worldviews that work for the destruction of the biblical worldview. Christians can take on alien worldviews and win because there is inherent in every alien humanistic worldview seeds of self-destruction. As Paul says, "They will not make further progress; for their folly will be obvious to all . . ." (2 Timothy 3:7-9). The Christian's war with alien worldviews is fought with unseen but immensely powerful weapons. We are told to "be strong in the Lord, and the strength of His might," to "put on the whole armor of God" (Ephesians 6:9-10), to "fight the good fight" (1 Timothy 1:18), to "suffer hardship . . . as a good soldier of Christ Jesus" (2 Timothy 2:3), and always to be "ready to make a defense to every one who asks you to give an account for the hope" that is in us (1 Peter 3:15). *War of the Worldviews* will equip you with the needed intellectual and spiritual ammunition to get the job done.

INTRODUCTION

Western culture is no longer seen as the child of the Reformation but rather an heir of the Enlightenment. Western culture is now Enlightenment culture, and the moral direction of our nation demonstrates that our reformational heritage has been discarded. The foundation of the Reformation was the Bible. Man, reason, and the world had meaning because God had decreed that they had meaning. Their significance was to be found in the context of a full-orbed biblical worldview where God is sovereign over all of life. The Enlightenment changed all of that. Man, reason, and the world had meaning because man so decreed. From this man-centered outlook a new world was to arise. No longer would man be restrained by the absolutes mandated by a sovereign God. By casting off the strictures of rules and regulations proclaimed from on high, a new world order would evolve.

> The utopian dream of the Enlightenment can be summed up by five words: reason, nature, happiness, progress, and liberty. It was thoroughly secular in its thinking. The humanistic elements which had risen during the Renaissance came to flood tide in the Enlightenment. Here was man starting from himself absolutely. And if the humanistic elements of the Renaissance stand in sharp contrast to the Reformation, the Enlightenment was in total antithesis to it. The two stood for and were based upon absolutely different things in an absolute way, and they produced absolutely different results.[1]

The shift from the ideals of reformational Christianity to Enlightenment humanism did not come overnight. Sides were chosen and ideological wars were waged.

Cotton Mather's history of early New England, *Magnalia Christi Americana*, or *The Great Achievement of Christ in America*, explained that "from the beginning of the Reformation in the English nation, there had always been a generation of godly men, desirous to pursue the reformation of religion, according to the Word of God. . . ." But in England, there were others with "power . . . in their hands" who desired "not only to stop the progress of the desired reformation but also, with innumerable vexation, to persecute those that most heartily wish well unto it." These early Christian settlers were "driven to seek a place for the exercise of the Protestant religion, according to the light of conscience, in the deserts of America." Their purpose was nothing less than to complete the Reformation, believing "that the first reformers never intended that what they did should be the absolute boundary of reformation."[2]

The Reformation, while still influencing many in the church, has taken a back seat to the Enlightenment worldview that spawned the French Revolution, Darwinism, Marxism, National Socialism (Nazism), and present-day secularism with all of its hideous effects. The spirit of the French Declaration of the Rights of Man (August 26, 1789) where "the Supreme Being" equaled "the sovereignty of the nation" (the general will of the people) has usurped the reformational worldview where sovereignty is God's alone. Whether it's the French "citizen," the Nazi *Volk*, the Marxist "proletariat," or "We the people," man rules in this new world order.

BACK TO BASICS

Man-centered worldviews oppose the biblical worldview at every point. Truth is turned into a lie (Romans 81:25); good becomes evil, and evil good (Isaiah 5:20); darkness is substituted for light, and light for darkness (Matthew 6:23; John 3:19; Isaiah 5:20); a "futile" and "depraved mind" (Ephesians 4:17; Romans 1:28) is preferred over a "renewed mind" (Romans 12:2).

The Bible tells us that those who parade their alien worldview "are without excuse. . . . For even though they knew God, they did not honor Him as God, or give thanks" (Romans 1:20-21). This rejection of the sovereign God leads to a downward spiral that begins with perverse thinking and degenerates into corrupt action. What was originally designed to be straight, man makes crooked by suppressing the truth in unrighteousness (Deuteronomy 32:5; Psalm 125:5; Proverbs 2:15; 3:32; 14:2; 17:20; 21:8; Philippians 2:15). This degeneration includes the thinking process and everything that follows.

INTRODUCTION

Step 1: Suppression of the truth (Romans 1:18): "who . . . repress and hinder the truth and make it inoperative" (Amplified Version).

Step 2: Intellectual futility (1:21): "they became futile in their speculations" (NASB).

Step 3: Spiritual darkness (1:21): "their senseless minds were darkened" (RSV).

Step 4: Incredible stupidity (1:22): "they boast of their wisdom, but they have made fools of themselves" (NEB).

Step 5: Deification of man and nature (1:23): they "changed the glory of the incorruptible God into an image made like corruptible man" (NKJV).

Step 6: Gross immorality (1:24-28): "God gave them up to uncleanness, in the lusts of their hearts, to dishonor their bodies" (NKJV); "vile passions" (ASV); "women exchanged natural relations for unnatural" (RSV); "men doing shameless things with men and getting an appropriate reward for their perversion" (Jerusalem Bible); "God has given them up to their own depraved reason" (NEB).

Step 7: Societal destruction (1:29-31): "This leads them to break all rules of conduct" (NEB); "they are steeped in all sorts of depravity, rottenness, greed and malice, and addicted to envy, murder, wrangling, treachery and spite" (Jerusalem Bible); "backbiters, haters of God, violent, proud, boasters, inventors of evil things, disobedient to parents" (NKJV); "senseless, faithless, heartless, ruthless" (NIV).

Step 8: Self-Denial (1:32): "Although they know God's righteous decree that those who do such things deserve death, they not only continue to do these very things but also approve of those who practice them" (NIV).

There is a direct relationship between what a person believes about the God of the Bible and the way a society formulates its ethical standards. Within our society there are numerous invading worldviews hell-bent on destroying the worldview of biblical Christianity: skepticism, modernism, agnosticism, atheism, liberalism, secular humanism, feminism, communism, leftism, empiricism, scientism, naturalism, hedonism, materialism, rationalism, mysticism, monism, deism, evolutionism, and a truckload of other "isms." While the labels have changed from one generation to another, they all have one thing in common: They are all at war with the God of the Bible.

1
PREPARING FOR BATTLE

> PHILOSOPHY I: (Prerequisite—five hours of sitting around doing nothing).
>
> Philosophy I is where you learn how the great thinkers of the past view man's existence, such as Descartes who said, "I think, therefore I am."
>
> It turns out he was right because he stopped thinking a while back, and now he no longer is![1]

WHEN entering a battle, you had better be prepared for the opposition. The following story will set the stage for what you will be learning in the *War of the Worldviews*.

It's ten o'clock at night. You're just leaving the library building. This is the third night this week that you've had to work on your research paper. You begin to walk toward your dorm. Out of the shadows of the alley behind the library building a man appears. He attempts to block your path. He appears to be about six feet, four inches tall, and probably weighs nearly two hundred fifty pounds. He's holding a knife with a ten-inch blade. He starts to walk toward you. The campus is deserted. Screaming for help would be fruitless. You know he wants to run you through. He's not after money. He wants your life.

You panic for a moment. But you remember that you're armed with a .45 service automatic. The instructor at the survival school warned you there would be nights like this.

Your sweat-drenched hand reaches into your coat to grasp the handle of the gun. The campus menace is just a few feet away. You shout to him in a weakened but confident voice:

"Stop! If you take one more step, I'll shoot!"

He laughs. Your calm turns to panic. Fear descends on you like a thick cloud. He shouts back to you,

"I don't believe in guns. And I certainly don't believe in .45 service automatics."

Fear has now gripped you like a vise. You put the gun down and allow the brute to slash you to pieces.

Of course, this student's reaction is absurd. Nobody in his right mind would cease to believe in the effectiveness of his weapon just because some brute didn't believe in it. Let's repeat the scene, but with a different twist.

The mugger steps out from the shadows of the alley to block your path. His knife blade reflects the parking lot lights, and the reflection catches your eye. The knife looks huge! You realize that he wants to slash you to pieces. You remain calm. You pull out your .45 service automatic and point it at the attacker. You shout to him in a confident voice,

"Stop! If you take one more step, I'll shoot!"

He laughs. He shouts back to you,

"I don't believe in guns. And I certainly don't believe in .45 service automatics."

With that last word he lunges at you with death in his eye. You make a believer out of him by emptying the clip of bullets into his lunging body.

In the second scenario the student had confidence in his weapon. The mugger's beliefs about the reliability of the .45 service automatic were irrelevant. His lack of belief in the power of the gun did not change

PREPARING FOR BATTLE

the gun's effectiveness. But the student's beliefs about the reliability of the service automatic were most relevant.

The student's life depended on his believing in the reliability of the weapon and the weapon's reliability to do what he was told it could do. The gun remained a gun, and the bullets remained bullets no matter what the mugger or student decided to believe. In order for the student to appropriate the potential of the gun, however, he had to unleash its power. The mugger was made epistemologically self-conscious* when the gun destroyed his unbelief.

> *Epistemology* is that part of philosophy which studies the nature, sources, and limits of human knowledge, as well as analyzing crucial concepts such as "truth," "belief," and "knowledge." To be *epistemologically self-conscious* means to become fully aware of the consistent implications and nature of your espoused position.

How many times have you been confronted by someone who said he didn't believe in God, the inerrancy and infallibility of the Bible, the divinity of Jesus Christ, miracles, the resurrection, and a whole host of other Bible doctrines? And when you were confronted with such unbelief, how many times were you cut to pieces because you acted as if the Bible were not true unless you could convince the skeptic of its truthfulness? How often do you in practice deny the faith or its power because a skeptic did not believe the Bible?

Let's take a final look at our mugging story. There is another methodology that a number of Christians use that is equally ineffective.

> The mugger sees your gun, but he is not convinced of its effectiveness. You consider his words of doubt and seek to persuade him that your gun is indeed effective. You tell him about your gun's fire power and the latest ballistic tests. You inform him of your weapon's accuracy and its reliability under adverse conditions. You even recite a list of experts who agree with your position. In the meantime, however, your attacker runs you through. You see, he doesn't believe your sources of information or considers them irrelevant. In his mind, they're just not reliable. They have no bearing on the present moment. He says your facts are all wrong. The experts? Well, they're just biased. They don't like

knives. They never have. Those in the "American Knife Throwers Association" have their own statistical data, and they refute the conclusions of the "National Gun Lovers of America."

DEFENDING THE FAITH

Your faith will be under constant attack by your peers, leaders in society, teachers, and media personalities. The assault will sometimes be overt. In the open attack, people will spend considerable time trying to refute the basic doctrines that every Christian holds to be true. They will begin by going to the source of the Christian's authority: the Bible. Once the Bible is set aside as true and reliable, all other doctrines are easily refuted since their veracity and credibility rest upon the Bible's authority. Some will use ridicule to discredit the Bible, while others will engage in a reasoned attack, using their own worldview to debunk the Christian worldview* piece by piece.

> **Worldview*: A network of elementary assumptions which are not verified by the procedures of natural science but in terms of which every aspect of man's experience and knowledge is interrelated and interpreted.

It's possible that you have never had your faith attacked in such an open way. Not everyone has experienced an open assault on the Christian faith, although the occurrence of these hostilities is on the rise. You may be convinced of the skeptic's reasons for rejecting the Bible and the Christian faith because you have never been taught how to defend what the Bible teaches. You have always been taught that the Bible is true, Jesus is God, man is a sinner, and there is an afterlife. Few Christians really question these basic beliefs. In today's culture however, all beliefs are open to criticism. Any belief system that claims to be *the* true system is doubly suspicious.

Preparing for the Confrontation

Like the man with the knife who confronted the college student with the gun, rival faiths are at work in the world. Often these rival faiths are consciously designed to stamp out all things Christian. Sometimes it's more subtle than that. Many people just ignore the Christian worldview.

―――――――― **PREPARING FOR BATTLE** ――――――――

Because the Christian worldview is rarely discussed in secular contexts (except to be ridiculed), the implicit message is to disregard Christianity as a serious option. Be on your guard. This is the most subtle and destructive tactic. If you can be convinced that you and your world can be defined and interpreted without reference to Jesus Christ and His Word, then Christianity has been rendered irrelevant, and you are on the road to skepticism or outright unbelief.

You may have tried to defend the faith, but found that the arguments were too difficult to handle. The next time your beliefs were attacked, you remained silent. You may have felt guilty after not standing up for Christ, but you really didn't know what to say. After hearing the same arguments leveled against Christianity time after time, the walls of your own belief system start to crumble. Skepticism begins to take over where faith once prevailed.

Maybe you have been taught that you should not defend the faith. You just "believe." Well, that doesn't work for long. It gets to you in time. Why believe in something if you cannot defend it? Anyway, the Bible tells us as Christians that we are responsible to defend the faith. Defending the faith is part of the Christian's life. It's not an option.

The best way to handle attacks by skeptics is to have worked out an apologetic* methodology. It's been said that the best defense is a good offense.

> *"*Apologetics* is the vindication of the Christian philosophy of life against the various forms of the non-Christian philosophy of life."[2]

Keep in mind that the Bible is like a loaded .45. The power to destroy all speculations raised up against the knowledge of God is inherent in God's Word.

> For though we walk in the flesh, we do not war according to the flesh, for the weapons of our warfare are not of the flesh, but divinely powerful for the destruction of fortresses. We are destroying speculations and every lofty thing raised up against the knowledge of God, and we are taking every thought captive to the obedience of Christ (2 Corinthians 10:3-5).

Yet many Christians either don't know how to use the Bible as a spiritual weapon or really don't believe it's very effective as a weapon. There are others who believe that the brutish worldviews of unbelief are valid if they simply deny the Bible and everything it stands for. However, a cogently presented, comprehensive, and consistent Christian worldview can stand up to any hostile belief system. But it takes work to understand how skeptics think, believe, and behave. And your job is not finished until you are always "ready to make a defense to every one who asks you to give a reason for the hope that is in you" (1 Peter 3:15). This is what apologetics is all about.

APOLOGETICS IN ACTION

Jesus and His disciples were constantly doing battle with opponents who were a lot meaner than today's secular bullies. However, Christ had much more at stake. He was not passive in the face of hostility and opposition. He met his attackers and systematically demolished their arguments against Him. Jesus won every argument. He sent the antagonists away mumbling to themselves. When the religious leaders of the day couldn't answer His arguments, they worked to have Him crucified. That's a rather extreme way to "win" an argument. But it's not so farfetched. Consider the creation/evolution and abortion controversies. Why isn't creation given a fair hearing in the public schools? Isn't the classroom the place where there is a free exchange of ideas? Aren't students exposed to *all* the options? Why do evolutionists work so hard to keep creationists out of the public school classrooms? Evolutionists are afraid of the competition. If they were really convinced that the arguments for their position are irrefutable, then they would welcome a defense by creationists just to show how wrong they are.

Why do pro-abortion groups fight to keep pro-life groups from showing what an abortion is really all about? Moreover, why is it that parents must be notified and permission must be sought for a minor to receive a flu shot, but parents are not told when their daughter is considering an abortion? If women knew the truth about abortion many of them would choose not to get one. This would jeopardize the multi-million dollar abortion business. Contrary positions are effectively silenced when those who hold the prevailing worldviews are allowed to regulate the discussion of evolution or abortion.

─────────── PREPARING FOR BATTLE ───────────

Jesus and the Skeptics

Jesus' defense of the faith against the skeptics, religious leaders, and legal profession had an effect on the people. After hearing Jesus the people began to question the bankrupt ideology of their leaders. First, Jesus' message began to turn the people away from the anti-supernatural worldview of the Sadducees. The Sadducees were the religious skeptics of the day. They didn't believe in the resurrection of the dead, for example. Upon hearing Jesus show the absurdity of the Sadducees' worldview, the people were "astonished at His teaching" (Matthew 22:33). Next up were leaders from the religious and legal professions: "But when the Pharisees heard that He had put the Sadducees to silence, they gathered themselves together. And one of them, a lawyer, asked Him a question, testing Him" (vv. 34-35). Jesus again defends the faith against unbelief. Their response? "And no one was able to answer Him a word, nor did anyone dare from that day on to ask Him another question" (v. 46).

Something had to be done with this troublemaker. It's no accident that Jesus was taken away to be tried secretly. The people would have turned on their leaders had they known what they had planned for Jesus. Jesus gave the people answers to life's most perplexing questions. Those in power were about to take it all away:

> Then the chief priests and the elders of the people were gathered together in the court of the high priest, named Caiaphas; and they plotted to seize Jesus by stealth, and kill Him. But they were saying, "Not during the festival, lest a riot occur among the people" (Matthew 26:3-5).

Jesus had challenged the perverted worldviews of both the Sadducees and Pharisees, and the people were on the verge of rejecting them, lock, stock, and barrel. In order to keep their public credibility intact and to hide the defects of their worldview, Jesus had to go.

NO APOLOGIES PLEASE

Instead of defending the faith against unbelief, many Christians actually apologize for what they believe. This is *not* Biblical apologetics. "Apologetics" does not mean saying you're sorry for being a Christian. "Apologetics" comes from a Greek word which means "to give or make a defense." It is closely related to the operations of a courtroom where defendants are called on to present their legal case against accusations of wrong-doing.

> The Greek word *apologia* (from which we derive the English word "apologetics") denotes a speech made in defense, a reply (especially in the legal context of a courtroom) made to an accusation. The word originated in the judicial operations of ancient Athens, but the word occurs several times in the New Testament as well. The difference between the Greek and Christian methods of apologetics can be illustrated by contrasting the *Apology* of Socrates (as Plato records it) with the approach of the apostle Paul, who described himself as "set for the defense (*apologia*) of the gospel."[3]

One of the earliest occurrences of the word is found when Socrates defended himself against the charge of atheism and corrupting the youth of Athens. For Socrates, "all of life and every thought had to be brought under obedience to the lordship of man's reason."[4] When Socrates dared to question the opinion of the gods, in effect he had dared to question the opinion of the State since the State had its own pantheon of recognized gods that no one could refuse to honor, not even the nation's philosopher *par excellence*. The Grecian State, as the modern secular State, was a religious institution. To espouse another god was more than treason; it was blasphemy. Exile or the death penalty was mandated for such an offense. Socrates, because of his belief in a divine calling, could not accept exile as an alternative to execution. Socrates' real sin was teaching that the individual, rather than man as a collective social whole, can be his own god, his own judge, determining for himself what is right, good, and true. This is what motivated his accusers to banish him. Instead of banishment, Socrates chose suicide.

Confronting Ignorance

The Apostle Paul found himself in a similar situation. Not only did he question the opinion of the gods, he called all men everywhere to repent and worship the one true God. Even reason* had to bow in submission before the God who created heaven and earth.

PREPARING FOR BATTLE

> *_Reason_ is man's intellectual ability, a tool for understanding ourselves and the world. Some people try to make it more than a tool, using man's independent intellect as a final authority or judge.

Paul went to the very heart of religious skepticism by confronting the Greek philosophers of Athens with their own ignorance. The Bible says that "his spirit was being provoked within him as he was beholding the city full of idols" (Acts 17:16). At this point, Paul went to work defending the faith, "reasoning in the synagogue with the Jews and the God-fearing Gentiles, and in the market place every day with those who happened to be present" (v. 17). Even "some of the Epicurean and Stoic philosophers were conversing with him" (v. 18). They, however, found that some of his views differed greatly from their own. He was accused of being a "proclaimer of strange demons" (v. 18). He was then brought to the Areopagus,[5] a public debating forum, so they could learn more about these new teachings. Here is a summary of Paul's defense in Acts 17:22-33:

1. He shows them that they are inherently religious, pointing out to them their objects of worship (v. 22).

Application: No person is without basic religious commitments. This point needs to be stressed throughout any defense of the faith. The issue is not between faith and reason, but between faith and faith. Since reason is only a *tool*, the issue is, Which faith-commitment (worldview) is employing the tool? The person who says that man's unaided "reason must be used to explain everything" has already made a faith commitment—to man's unaided ability to reason independent of God. He must believe that unaided reason can explain everything before he will use that same unaided reason to prove its ability.

2. He notes that even the Athenians admit that they do not have all the facts, pointing out an altar that they erected "TO AN UNKNOWN GOD" (v. 23).

Application: The skeptic wants to be the judge as to whether God exists and what kind of God exists. But how can he ever be sure that *his* God exists? How can he be sure that his *kind* of God exists? Not having all the facts limits the dogmatism of the unbeliever. Ultimately, when we do not have personal observations of all the facts, the argument will come down to a faith-commitment because all of us are forced to trust some other authority outside ourselves which interprets the observed facts and reveals what we do not observe. Paul's point is that God is that outside Observer.

3. He shows them a way out of their ignorance by describing the true God who is "Lord of heaven and earth" (v. 24).

Application: The Bible never leaves the skeptic in his ignorance. The skeptic is left with nothing if he can be shown that his entire belief system is based upon unknowns. He can't be sure of anything. But the Christian's position establishes that because God is "Lord of heaven and earth," we can make sense of the world. Randomness does not characterize the universe. "Christianity provides an explanation even for our ignorance. We may be ignorant because of our finiteness as human beings. Yet, we can be sure that if an answer is to be found it must be done by dependence on the revelation of God."[6] That revelation is reliable because it comes from a God who is "Lord of heaven and earth."

4. He shows them that the true God is in need of nothing, "since He Himself gives to all life and breath and all things" (v. 25).

Application: Trusting in the God of the Bible means trusting Someone who is able to sustain us in life and death. There is no assurance of this in the skeptic's worldview. He either depends on himself or he looks to other belief systems to satisfy his spiritual hunger. But there is no assurance that any of these can supply what man needs: purpose, love, hope, fulfillment, a sense of meaning and belonging, the relief of guilt, and life after death. Only an independent God who is in need of nothing can supply what others cannot supply for themselves.

5. He shows them that there is no way to escape the presence and government of God since He has "determined their appointed times, and the boundaries of their habitation" (v. 26). Neither can they escape the implications of God's providence, "For in *Him* we live and move and exist" (vv. 26-28).

Application: There is no escaping God. The breath that God gives man to enable him to speak is used to deny Him. A personal God who sees and judges what man does is banned by those who want to live independent, autonomous* lives, free from the restrictions of a holy God.

---

*Autonomous: Characterized by self-sufficiency or independence from outside authority (especially God's authority). The word is derived from two Greek words, *autos* (self) and *nomos* (law).

PREPARING FOR BATTLE

God is defined or rationalized out of existence. When King David was confronted by Nathan with his sin, David's confession brought him back to reality: God sees and judges all things. There is no escape from the gaze of God: "Against Thee, Thee only, I have sinned, and done what is evil in Thy sight, so that Thou art justified when Thou dost speak, and blameless when Thou dost judge" (Psalm 51:4a).

Here David acknowledges the reality of that guilt and notes two very important factors. First he notes that the sin is *ever* before him. It hounds him and pursues him. He sees it wherever he goes. He cannot rid himself of the memory. Like Lady Macbeth, the spot is indelible. Second, he notes that he has done evil in the sight of God. Thus, David not only sees his sin but he realizes it has not escaped the notice of God.[7]

A Biblically transcendent* God—a God who sees, acts, and judges—cannot be allowed in the universe by those who deny an absolute law they must obey or a deity to whom they must submit.

> *Transcendent*: The quality of originating beyond, or exceeding, man's temporal experience. Biblical transcendence should not be confused with the notion that God has nothing to do with the world.

6. Paul shows the Athenians that God is no longer overlooking "the times of ignorance." He "is now declaring to men that all everywhere should repent" (v. 30), that is, change their *minds* about the God of the Bible, their sin, and Jesus Christ, their Redeemer.

Application: Ultimately, the defense of the faith is not about knowledge of the facts but about ethics, that is, how we act. The reason that man seeks to escape from God by rationalizing argumentation is that he has sins to hide and a Judge he doesn't want to face. Most arguments that seek to deny God or the validity of the Christian message are simply smoke screens to obscure the real issue: Man is a sinner who "suppresses the truth in unrighteousness" (Romans 1:18).

7. He shows them that God has "fixed a day in which He will judge the world in righteousness through a man He has appointed" (v. 31).

Application: The skeptic cannot remain neutral when he is confronted with the gospel. Refusal to decide for Christ with a wait-and-see attitude does not absolve him of his guilt and eventual judgment. Straddling the fence will not save him. Judgment is coming. Even if we do not "win" our argument with the skeptic, we must always warn him of the consequences of unbelief. When the arguments are laid aside, the question still remains: "What do you think of Jesus Christ?," and "What does He think of *you*?"

8. He shows them that God has furnished proof to all men that this is all true "by raising Him from the dead" (v. 31).

Application: The resurrection of Jesus from the dead is incredible but not in terms of the Christian worldview where God is Lord of heaven and earth and supplies to all life and breath, and all things. The resurrection is a confirmation of God's power and a vindication of His grace. The resurrection is taken for granted as a premise by Paul. It proves that Jesus is the final judge. Paul does not argue for the resurrection as a conclusion. He presents it as fact.

"Now when they heard of the resurrection of the dead, some began to sneer, but others said, 'We shall hear you again concerning this'" (v. 32). This is the essence of defending the faith. Some will reject the faith because what you tell them does not fit within the framework of their worldview. Those who rejected the faith at this point did so because their starting point was contrary to the Christian faith. Their worldview was constructed on a foundation of unknowns: unknown gods, unknown forces, unknown random facts, unjustifiable universal laws, and unverified claims to authority. Such ignorance God will no longer tolerate. Such a worldview is destined for judgment. It can only lead to skepticism, mysticism, or irrationality. The words to the youthful student Timothy are appropriate advice for any Christian:

> O Timothy, guard what has been entrusted to you, avoiding worldly and empty chatter and the opposing arguments of what is falsely called "knowledge"—which some have professed and thus gone astray from the faith. Grace be with you (2 Timothy 6:21).

Greg Bahnsen sums up the Christian's apologetic task.

> Until the Holy Spirit regenerates the sinner and brings him to repentance, his presuppositions will remain unaltered. And as long as the unbeliever's presuppositions are unchanged, a proper acceptance and understanding of the good news of Christ's historical resurrection will be impossible. The Athenian philoso-

PREPARING FOR BATTLE

phers had originally asked Paul for an account of his doctrine of resurrection. After his reasoned defense of the hope within him and his challenge to the philosophers' presuppositions, a few were turned around in their thinking. But many refused to correct their presuppositions, so that when Paul concluded with Christ's resurrection they ridiculed and mocked.

Acceptance of the facts is governed by one's most ultimate assumptions, as Paul was well aware. Paul began his apologetic with God and His revelation. The Athenian philosophers began their dispute with Paul in an attitude of cynical unbelief about Christ's resurrection. . . .

Paul knew that the explanation of their hostility to God's revelation (even though they evidenced an inability to escape its forcefulness) was to be found in their desire to exercise control over God (e.g., v. 29) and to avoid facing up to the fact of their deserved punishment before the judgment seat of God (v. 30). They secretly hoped that ignorance would be bliss, and so preferred darkness to light (John 3:19-20).[8]

RIVAL FAITHS AT WORK

The Biblical faith is dogmatic. It makes some absolute statements about fundamental doctrines: God exists, man was created, sin has infected this world, man is accountable to God, and Jesus Christ is our only hope in life and in death. These declarations are not acceptable to the secular world which is not in the business of dealing in absolutes,* at least in absolutes that make man accountable to God.

> *An *absolute* is a statement whose truth is not conditioned by qualification or limitations (such as subjective bias or cultural trends and conditioning).

The goal of the secular worldview is to strip self-proclaimed Christians of their absolute worldview and to clothe them with the robe of criticism and relativism. No view of life is sacred. All views but one are equal. Secularism has only one dogma: criticism. It has only one absolute: Nothing is absolute (all is relative). This view is prevalent on college campuses:

What makes the university unique is the centrality of criticism and debate in every facet of its functioning. The discussion is open, and all the members of the community, i.e, the inquirers, are entitled, in fact obliged, to participate. All members of the community, but most importantly the leadership, are made accountable by the checks and balances of constant peer review. This is not some occasional occurrence; it is the way of life in the university. No claim, issue, or position is insulated from critical inquiry. The university certainly has other important goals, but they are all subordinate to this one.[9]

As Christians we do not want to accept every new idea or every interpretation of reality without a degree of healthy skepticism. Questions should be asked. Mistrust of dogma is helpful, if put in the context of a reliable worldview in terms of which criticism has a foundation on which to stand. There must be standards for our criticism. But for our "enlightened" culture all absolutes are exposed to criticism. Are we to hold the existence of God up for criticism by "peer review"? What "checks and balances" govern the "community" engaged in the criticism? Consider what it means to maintain that "no claim, issue, or position is insulated from critical inquiry" and that all values "are all subordinate to this one." The claim that God is the sovereign ruler of heaven and earth and that man is accountable to Him in thought, word, and deed "is subordinate" to critical inquiry. The men of Athens are still with us.

How did this happen? What went wrong? There was a day when the general society accepted that all of life should be viewed through the interpretive and corrective lens of Scripture. God was considered to be the foundation of knowledge and final authority in life, not some spurious and seemingly neutral community of "critical inquirers." In actuality, even our modern culture still stands on that earlier foundation (since there is no other way to gain knowledge), although it rarely acknowledges it. The philosophical walls are crumbling, however, and it is only a matter of time until the entire edifice comes crashing down. The foundation will still be there, but it will take a new generation of Christians to rebuild the walls.

The only reason secular institutions can do any positive work today is that they haven't been consistent with their own bankrupt worldview. Consistency would only lead to despair, ignorance, and social chaos. When the world wakes up one morning and fully comprehends what it

PREPARING FOR BATTLE

means to live without God, life as we know it will no longer exist. The savage will replace civilized man, the image-bearer of God, and chaos will be the result. Of course, there is another avenue. The world might return to the One who originally gave it life.

But at the heart of the secular critical agenda there still remains a more fundamental problem: Man and the universe in which he lives have been reduced to machine-like status, to something less than what they were created to be. With God slowly pushed to the edge of the universe, man is no longer a "little lower than the angels" (Psalm 8:5); he is only a little higher than the apes.

BUILDING A SPIRITUAL ARSENAL

The importance of being prepared to succeed in an environment hostile to the gospel is nothing new to the Christian. And I suspect that most Christians agree that spiritual preparation must accompany career-related preparation. But how do you prepare yourself spiritually for entering the marketplace of ideas? What is *spiritual* preparedness? Why must you be spiritually prepared? Isn't academic preparation enough? Besides, what does education have to do with religion anyway? Aren't they separate and distinct areas of life and study?

These fundamental questions must be answered. Religion, the fundamental belief system that all men and women use to interpret reality, cannot be separated from anything, let alone education or career. All people choose something outside themselves to interpret reality. This external standard is spiritual in nature. Keep in mind that when we talk about "spiritual," we do not mean only the world that exists beyond our senses. We are also talking about our relationship with God through Jesus Christ, which leads to complete devotion—heart, mind, soul, and body—to Him. When the Bible talks, for example, about "the spiritual man," it's usually talking about the guidance, direction, and regulation of a person's life. A Spiritual person is someone whose relationship with Jesus Christ shapes the way he or she believes, thinks, and acts—who is led by *God's* Spirit. Thus, the following questions test your "spirituality."

What *standard* is *guiding* your decisions?

What *principle* is *directing* your view of life?

What *laws* are *regulating* your behavior?

Spirituality is inseparable from first principles of ethical behavior. Ethics has to do with deciding what is right and wrong, good and evil, just and unjust. There are always unseen precepts that stand behind our thoughts and actions. They are always present, and they give meaning to our concept of reality. In Biblical language, to be Spiritual means "to be guided and motivated by the Holy Spirit. It means obeying His commandments as recorded in the Scriptures. The Spiritual man is not someone who floats in midair and hears eerie voices. The Spiritual man is the man who does what the Bible says (Romans 8:4-8)."[10]

Even those who deny the Christian faith are religious. They are just as much controlled by implicit internal principles as the most devout Christian. Their spiritual first principles, however, are contrary to the Bible's spiritual principles. This is why the Bible tells us not to "believe every spirit, but test the spirits to see whether they are from God" (1 John 4:1). There is a spirit behind every decision. Is it the spirit of man or the Spirit of God?

> Now we have received, not the spirit of the world, but the Spirit who is from God, that we might know the things freely given to us by God, which things we also speak, not in words taught by human wisdom, but in those taught by the Spirit, combining spiritual thoughts with spiritual words. But a natural man does not accept the things of the Spirit of God; for they are foolishness to him, and he cannot understand them, because they are spiritually appraised. But he who is spiritual appraises all things, yet he himself is appraised by no man. For who has known the mind of the Lord, that he should instruct Him? But we have the mind of Christ (1 Corinthians 2:12-16).

The religious commitments of those who reject the wisdom of God in Christ can go in two directions. At first, those who reject Biblical spiritual guidance deny that there is a spiritual reality beyond what they can observe. They say that there isn't anything more to life than eating, drinking, sleeping, dying, and then nothing more beyond the grave. For them there is nothing beyond what they experience with their senses. This very premise, however, is something which goes *beyond* what anybody can experience with his senses! How do they really *know*?

But this denial usually doesn't last very long. It is a transitional position. Eventually, they realize that this interpretation of reality cannot satisfy them. Then, if they don't turn to Christ and the guidance offered

PREPARING FOR BATTLE

through the Holy Spirit and His Word, they turn to any number of spiritual substitutes. Some become self-conscious, consistent humanists* or atheists, believing that man should be his own god.

> *Humanism* is the view that man is the highest value and authority in terms of knowledge or behavior (rejecting any transcendent reality or revelation).

Most don't go that far. Instead, they operate with an inconsistent, rough-and-ready view of the world that excludes God and exalts man. Though they are not very consistent, they are humanists in their basic orientation. Some become self-conscious Satanists. Between these two extremes there are all types of spiritual counterfeits.

Here is one striking example of an opposing and deeply religious faith that is designed to supplant Christianity. Notice that all the forms of religion are present:

> I am convinced that *the battle for humankind's future must be waged and won in the public school classroom* by teachers who correctly perceive their role as the proselytizers of a new faith: a religion of humanity that recognizes and respects the spark of what theologians call divinity in every human being. These teachers must embody the same selfless dedication as the most rabid fundamentalist preachers, for they will be ministers of another sort, utilizing a classroom instead of a pulpit to convey humanist values in whatever subject they teach, regardless of the educational level–preschool day care or large state university. *The classroom must and will become an arena of conflict between the old and the new – the rotting corpse of Christianity, together with all its adjacent evils and misery, and the new faith of humanism, resplendent in its promise of a world in which the never-realized Christian ideal of "love thy neighbor" will be finally achieved.*[11]

Therefore, the question is not: Are you religious and does your religion affect the way you think and act? Rather, the question ought to be: What is your religion and how is it governing the way you think and act? As the above quotation makes clear, education is one vehicle by which the new faith is implemented. The task is to exclude all contrary faiths, especially Christianity. Man-centered religious principles should be implemented to define and interpret the world.

A Man-Centered Substitute

A denial of the Christian faith,* therefore, does not mean a denial of faith itself.

> *Faith*, contrary to common conceptions, does not mean abandoning intellect for feeling, experience, or intuition. To have "faith" is to believe something and live in terms of it.

Abandoning faith in the God of Scripture means choosing another faith-commitment. A shift takes place, from a God-centered, God-created, and God-interpreted universe to a man-centered, man-interpreted, man-controlled universe. All of life is explained in terms of man:

1. Man is the center of the new faith. *Conclusion*: Man defines what is real.

2. There is no will greater than man's will. *Conclusion*: Right and wrong are determined by man and man alone.

3. This world is all there is. *Conclusion*: There is no God to worship and obey, no heaven to consider, and no hell to fear. Even if these do exist, man can never know for sure.

4. There is no spiritual dimension to man's existence, nothing beyond the world of physical experience that can give meaning to life. By observing and drawing conclusions from what man hears, sees, and experiences, man gains all the "meaning" available in life. *Conclusion*: If it cannot be measured with scientific instruments, then it is not real.

5. If there is a spiritual dimension to life, man defines it, creates it, and lives in terms of his own definitions. *Conclusion*: All religions are valid except any religion that says that not all religions are valid; therefore, Christianity is banned because it is exclusive in what it claims to be true.

Christians tend to believe that a denial of the God of the Bible means a denial of religion altogether. This is never true. Even the most ardent atheist is religious.*

PREPARING FOR BATTLE

> **Religion* involves our ultimate commitments regarding the nature of reality and knowledge, about man's place in the universe, how we should live, and the meaning of life. A religious person does not have to believe in a personal god. Anything will do.

An atheist shifts his worship from the true God to himself or to some other man-made object of worship, such as power, money, or fame. Of course, he may not admit this. In fact, he may deny it by claiming that he is an atheist (*a* means no; *theos* means god). Yet, he lives by a new set of religious principles on a daily basis. It's not only what a man *says* he believes, but also how he acts which shows what his basic commitments (beliefs) are. But there are some who understand the implications of denying God, and how this denial shifts religious sentiment to autonomous man. Consider this letter from a self-professed atheist:

1. I am my own authority (my own god). You choose to follow another authority while I do not.

2. I firmly believe in moral anarchy (to determine my own morality and to deny you and your kind the authority to impose yours on me).

3. I deny the existence of any objective "god's law."

4. I don't have to justify my ethical rules to you or to anyone else, so long as my acts hurt no one but myself.[12]

You can't be much more specific than this. While this man denies the existence of one God, he considers himself to be an adequate substitute. He now makes the rules, and he will work to bring the world under the terms of his new law-order. This is an obvious inconsistency. The "rule" that "we must not hurt anyone else" is taken as an objective to be imposed on all of us!

The Neutrality Myth

God always requires us to make a decision, either for Him or against Him (see Matthew 12:30). There is no middle ground. Neutrality is not an option for either the Christian or the non-Christian. On judgment day, those who have not turned to Christ will not be able to maintain their innocence by claiming that they did not speak against Christ.

The neutrality myth has been used by secularists to keep a Christian perspective of the world out of the arena of intellectual thought. Unfortunately, many Christians have fallen in the trap by assuming that a subject can be studied without any reference to religious presuppositions. Christians are told, "You can develop your own *personal religious* convictions, but you cannot bring these *personal religious* convictions to the classroom. You must be neutral like your professor."

The assumption is that those who are making the request are being neutral. But they are not. Everybody looks at the world in nonneutral terms. Some worldview—a set of formulated presuppositions—will be used to evaluate every fact and idea that is presented. Everybody evaluates life from a certain religious point of view. Even the atheist is not neutral. His analysis of the world is based on the presupposition that there is no God. In fact, denying God's Word a place in intellectual discussions because it assumes a religious presupposition is not neutrality. It's an action *against* God and His Word.

The secularists will allow Christians a privatized Christianity, insisting that religion need not play a part in academic and historic intellectual discussion. In many cases Christians willingly accommodate their secular antagonists by accepting the neutrality myth. But, for a Christian to adopt neutrality is to think like a humanist.

Secularists and, unfortunately, a majority of Christians believe that the world's problems can be solved through technical expertise without any regard for divine intervention. This view teaches that special revelation has little or nothing to say about "secular" things like education, politics, and law. It teaches that an unbeliever, without Scripture, is capable of developing equitable laws, a sound educational philosophy, and a just political system. This is the myth of neutrality. What happens when neutrality is claimed? God and His Word have no voice in decision making. Man becomes the law-maker.

For Christians to adopt the neutrality myth is to give all opposing (non-Christian) ideologies dominance. Of course, ideas are then translated into action and public policy. Belief systems will be worked out in real life. If biblically based values are not dominant, some other set of values will be. Jesus requires Christians to be "the salt of the earth" and the "light of the world," which means we must interact with—and influence—public institutions. This will mean starting on the right presuppositional foot. The Christian's responsibilities is to begin with the inerrant and infallible Word of the Sovereign Lord of heaven and earth.

CONCLUSION

The abandonment of God is never complete or comprehensive. When the God of Scripture is abandoned an idol is substituted, usually some man-made philosophy.[13] As G. K. Chesterton observed, when people cease to believe in God they do not stop believing. What is worse, they believe in anything, no matter how foolish.

We are experiencing the conflict of two rival faiths—Christianity that teaches God is Sovereign over all He has created, and the variety of worldviews that teach that Man is sovereign over all that has evolved up to this moment. This was brought home to me as I was picketing with a group of pro-life activists at an Atlanta abortuary. We were singing a number of hymns in our march around the building. As we sang "A Mighty Fortress is our God," I could hear one of the staff members of the abortuary say, "I guess we ought to sing 'A Mighty Fortress is our Man.'" He understood the nature of the battle. The issue is God or Man. According to the man-centered faiths, man believes he is in control of the evolutionary process. Man works to determine the future.

> Through billions of years of blind mutation, pressing against the shifting walls of their environment, microbes finally emerged as man. We are no longer blind; at least we are beginning to be conscious of what has happened and of what may happen. From now on, evolution is what we make it.[14]

The man-centered views of life want every vestige of Christianity expunged from every nook and cranny of the universe. As history shows us, such worldviews breed totalitarianism, enslavement, and the wholesale slaughter of untold millions. The State becomes the new god.

When man is left to himself (without God) to be his own authority, this leads either to anarchy (every man is his own law) or Statism (collective man makes the laws). Since anarchy destroys civilizations (the individual's personal peace and affluence) the tendency in history is for anarchistic periods to give way to totalitarianism.

Is your faith strong enough to survive the attack from those who are hostile to everything the Bible stands for? You must be ready.

2
WORLDVIEWS IN CONFLICT

There is no longer a Christian mind.

It is commonplace that the mind of modern man has been secularized. For instance, it has been deprived of any orientation towards the supernatural. Tragic as this fact is, it would not be so desperately tragic had the Christian mind held out against the secular drift. But unfortunately the Christian mind has succumbed to the secular drift with a degree of weakness and nervelessness unmatched in Christian history. It is difficult to do justice in words to the complete loss of intellectual morale in the twentieth-century Church.[1]

THE world is a spiritual and intellectual war zone. Few Christians expect to encounter outspoken hostility toward the Christian faith. Non-Christians, however, will be relentless in their attack. Let's look at the academic world where the battle lines are clearly drawn. At the high school level, most teachers who are hostile to the Christian worldview are somewhat restrained in their animosity because they must answer to parent/teacher groups and school boards. The conflict escalates at the university level where there is little accountability and "academic freedom" supposedly rules.

Many college students think of the classroom as an open forum for the honest exchange of ideas. The pursuit of knowledge is thought to be a neutral enterprise. Supposedly there is a give and take atmosphere where, given enough of the facts, any student can come to the correct conclusions about any subject.

But is this true in practice? Is the university free and open to all ideas? Consider recent events at Northwestern University near Chicago. In the September 1986 issue of *Commentary*, Joseph Epstein, editor of *The American Scholar*, described the case of Barbara Foley, an avowedly Marxist professor of English at Northwestern. Foley is a strong supporter of InCAR, the International Committee Against Racism, a student group with well-known Marxist sympathies. Foley and InCAR gained widespread attention during a visit by Adolfo Calero, a leader of the Nicaraguan resistance. Before Calero spoke, Foley took the stage, announced herself as a member of InCAR, and said that "Adolfo Calero was a monster" and that "Calero had the blood of thousands on his hands and no respect for the rights to life and free speech of the people he helped slaughter with the CIA's help," and therefore that "He had no right to speak that night." She concluded, "We are not going to let him speak" and he "should feel lucky to get out alive."

Foley's lies and rhetoric aroused the students. Epstein writes:

> When Adolfo Calero arrived there was a great deal of chanting and shouting in opposition to his presence. His talk was delayed some ten or fifteen minutes. Before he could begin someone—not Barbara Foley—rushed to the stage and threw a red liquid on him. The liquid had been variously described as paint and as animal blood. At this point, with a good deal of shouting in the hall, Adolfo Calero, his suit coat bespattered with the red liquid, was led from the hall by security men and did not speak that evening. Barbara Foley acknowledges joining in the chanting during the tumult. A witness claims that she also shouted "the only way to get anything done would be to kill him [Calero]," though she and another witness, a graduate student who is also a member of InCAR, deny that she said this.[2]

The modern "free" university rarely tolerates contrary opinion. Other worldviews? "Well, we discuss them all here." The Christian world view? "That's not really an option anymore. It's more in the area of superstition." The creation-evolution debate? "What debate? Evolution has been proven to be true."

At Tennessee Tech in Cookeville, Josh McDowell, a popular speaker at Christian and non-Christian colleges and universities, was barred from campus because of the religious content of his message.[3] Some state colleges and universities now prohibit the use of its campus facilities for any meeting where religious worship takes place. A number of colleges have a ban on outside religious speakers.

The reason for the bans? Religion is a *private* affair. As soon as religion is involved in *public* life, the State must enforce the infamous and mythological constitutional "church/state separation"[4] doctrine. Religious expression, according to the prevailing view, is restricted to the mind and designated areas like churches and homes. You are within the law as long as you only *think* religious thoughts.

The Jigsaw Worldview

Modern educational philosophy sees life as a gigantic jigsaw puzzle. Man's job is to find all the pieces and put the puzzle together. But there's a catch. Man can never gather all the facts. And even if he could, what pattern would he follow to put all the pieces in the right places? Professors will tell their students that they do not interpret the facts; they only discover them and make them known. The facts, we are told, speak for themselves. Consistant secularists maintain that they can have no confidence that there is a "pattern" to the facts (a grand scheme of things). All meaning is therefore imposed by man's mind. Meaning is man's creation.

This is like expecting that after an hour of shaking a box of jigsaw puzzle pieces, the puzzle would be put together. But, of course, it can never happen. Someone must show you how the pieces fit. An already-established design must be followed. If not God's design, then the chaotic worldview of autonomous man will be the determining factor. Non-Christians will always try to show you how the pieces fit. And if the pieces don't fit, you will be told that they either belong to some other puzzle, or they don't exist.

YOU AND YOUR WORLDVIEW

What is a worldview? A worldview is the way a person looks at and evaluates the world in which he or she lives. This evaluation includes what a person sees, feels, and believes. Questions concerning values and ultimate reality are answered through worldviews. Worldviews embrace the daily operations of life, whether recognized or not:

> *The intellectual life* (what they believe is true about themselves and their place in history); *the physical* (how they treat or mistreat their bodies by eating, sleeping, and exercising); *the social* (how they interact with friends and enemies, the rich and

the poor, the strong and the weak); *the economic* (why they work and how they spend their wages); and *the moral* (what ethical guidelines and obligations direct their thinking about justice and issues such as abortion and euthanasia).⁵

Worldviews consist of presuppositions* that give us a refocused picture of the world. Because of sin, man and his world are distorted. "As we study God's Word we can progressively gain a clearer understanding of what the world is like, and how we can serve God more effectively in it."⁶

---

*A *presupposition* is an elementary assumption, basic commitment, or foundational perspective in terms of which particular experiences and events are interpreted.

A WORLDVIEW FRAMEWORK

While there are many worldviews, there are certain characteristics that form a framework for all of them. You can determine a person's worldview by asking certain questions:

1. What is he using to interpret the facts? What is he using as his worldview? What are his fundamental beliefs about life?
2. How consistent is his worldview? How consistent, for example, is a professor who says that God does not exist? Are there *any* absolutes? Why? Are there any right or wrong answers? If so, why? Does this include tests? Mathematical formulas? The rules of logic?
3. What are the practical implications of believing a certain worldview? What will it mean for me personally and the world in general?

These questions and many more reveal what constitutes an operating worldview. Let's look at these characteristics in detail.

I. Worldviews Consist of Presuppositions

Have you ever gotten into an argument with someone over a political, ethical, or religious question and found that you just could not come to an agreement? Maybe you saw a movie together and could not agree on what it was all about. You saw the same movie. Then why the disagreement? The disagreement could be the result of two things. First, the difference could be one of perspective. Everyone sees things in a

WORLDVIEWS IN CONFLICT

unique way, because of his experiences and interests. One of you might have watched the movie with an eye to the symbolism. Another might have watched looking for philosophical ideas in the movie. Someone might have evaluated it in terms of its story line. These are differences of perspective. There is nothing wrong with having different perspectives. At this level, every perspective would give a part of the whole. They could all be correct. A discussion would help you see different dimensions of the movie and enrich your understanding of it.

Second, your disagreement could be more fundamental. Your disagreement about the movie could be a disagreement about *presuppositions*, those fundamental values that we use to interpret life. For example, you might have watched *Tender Mercies*, a movie about how the grace of God transforms the life of an aging country singer. If you are a Christian, you would be able to understand and identify with the movie's themes. You would conclude that it gives a true picture of reality. An unbeliever, on the other hand, might see it as a naive fairy tale about something that can never happen in the real world. More likely, he will see nothing but despair. The man's daughter died in a senseless automobile accident. For him, there are no answers in life. Believing in a sovereign God is absurd. If this is the kind of disagreement you have, your disagreement really comes down to presuppositions about what life is all about. While you saw the same movie, and you discussed the same questions, you saw things differently. But these differences of opinion affect eternal things.

In other words, disagreements about issues often result from a more fundamental disagreement about the evaluating principles people use to see the facts. Now, if this type of disagreement is present in personal relationships where in many cases the issues being discussed are not very significant, what will happen when you enter the larger marketplace of ideas where life's most perplexing issues are discussed? Conflict.

Presuppositions, our basic commitments, influence all our thinking. They are the building blocks of a worldview. Presuppositions are the spectacles through which you, your peers, and your employees will view the facts. They are, by definition, more basic than our particular judgments and applied interpretations. Presuppositions govern the way all of us think and act, and they have significant personal and cultural ramifications. They determine the *ultimate* standards and so cannot be proved by anything else "more ultimate." An ultimate presupposition is "a belief over which no other takes precedence."[7] They are "proved" by the impossibility of the contrary. There are no answers to life's most fundamental questions if the God of the Bible is left out of the thinking process. We could not think or live without thinking presuppositionally.

> Human existence is structured by ideas. [Sets of] presuppositions and ideas [make up] worldviews—the grid through which we view the world. More importantly, a person's presuppositions are the basis upon which he or she acts.
>
> People are more than a mere product of their environment. Men and women project their inward thoughts out into the external world where, in fact, their thoughts affect their environment. Ideas, thus, have consequences, which can be productive or destructive—depending upon their basis or foundation.
>
> Ideas are, then, not neutral. Their mere existence implies impact.[8]

But it's not enough to have presuppositions. You must have the correct presuppositions. If you are wrong about your fundamental values—your presuppositions, the grid through which you evaluate life—then all your facts will be out of alignment. What you believe to be real could in fact be an illusion or a distortion. So then, presuppositions must be more than mere opinion. They cannot be arbitrary or subjective. For example, the ultimate "sin" of a "scholar" is inconsistency and arbitrariness. Yet this is precisely what the modern university condones and encourages regarding ultimate commitments: There are no fixed rules or standards, yet a professor will demand rules and standards be followed in scholarly research.

Without presuppositions, thinking is impossible. For example, if you do not begin with the presupposition that the God of the Bible exists, then some other presupposition will replace it. Without the God of the Bible, however, the explanation for the origin and maintenance of the universe degenerates into chaos, chance, unpredictability, and impersonalism. Without God, all things are possible and permissible including theft, slavery, rape, murder, and genocide. And there is no one to tell us that these things are evil. At the same time, there is no way to study science because the scientific method requires predictability in experimentation. Only an orderly universe designed by a God of law can effectively work for the scientist.

The Bible assumes God's existence. There is no attempt to prove His existence. No other type of world can be imagined without the existence of the Triune God of Scripture: "In the beginning, God created the heavens and the earth" (Genesis 1:1). Creation testifies to the reality of God.

Presuppositions, or worldviews, influence and shape all other convictions and are the prime interpreters of the facts. This bears repeating because most students rarely get beyond the facts to the belief system that is being used to interpret those "facts."

2. Worldviews Claim to be Unified

Worldviews work to unify thinking and the many new experiences that confront you daily. Without a predetermined system of evaluation for new information, facts would float unrelated to anything and be without meaning. If you did not think in terms of presuppositions, every new fact would have to be studied and examined as if no other fact had ever existed. All new facts would be independent facts. Your outlook would be fragmented. You would not have confidence that any single fact could ever be related to other facts. The Bible presents a unified view of reality that is consistent, rational, logical, and coherent.

There is a reason why schools of higher learning were first described as *uni*versities. Knowledge was thought to be unified. There was an attempt to have basic presuppositions govern all fields of knowledge. As a student moved from science to mathematics to political science to theology, he took with him a set of presuppositions which unified life and experience. There was little tension between the various disciplines. Such a view no longer governs educational pursuits at the university level. All is possible and permissible, except, of course, the Christian worldview. Rushdoony writes:

> In the 20th century, educators have spoken of the university at times as a *multiversity*, having room for a variety of ideas and faiths. The teaching of witchcraft, astrology, and related concepts by some schools is related to this concept of the multiversity. High schools in a major city have introduced yoga and palmistry. If the world is a multiverse, then all things are permissible except a sovereign God and a universal law-order. Hence our polytheistic world is tolerant of almost every kind of belief except orthodox Christianity. A universal law-order and a sovereign God rule out the possibility of a polytheistic multiverse. But, because the sovereign and triune God of Scripture rules, there is no multiverse but rather a universe and a unified law-order.[9]

When evaluating worldviews, you must evaluate them in terms of their inner consistency and cogency. Do the various aspects of the worldview and practices associated with it agree with each other? One would expect those who believe in saving the whales to support the issue of the sanctity of the unborn. If they believe that a whale or baby seal is important, then we have a right to ask them why they should not also emphasize the protection of defenseless *human* life.

If someone says *all* human laws and generalizations are relative, he will have to explain the absolutism and the universality of the laws of logic. If someone says there are no ethical absolutes, he will have to explain why falsifying lab reports in scientific research is forbidden or why cheating on exams is unacceptable to him.

3. Worldviews are Constructed to be Coherent

Worldviews aim to make the facts of experience fit together. New ideas often disturb entrenched worldviews. Observations or claims that do not fit a person's adopted worldview are often discarded as non-facts or determined to be irrelevant to the discussion. For example, when Jesus was raised from the dead, the chief priests realized that they could explain the event away by claiming that the whole story was fabricated by Jesus' disciples. The soldiers who reported the resurrection were given large sums of money to say, "His disciples came by night and stole Him away while we were asleep" (Matthew 28:13).

What about those who knew the truth about the resurrection? Did they become believers in light of the resurrection evidence? Not all of them. Many were content to dismiss the obvious testimony of eyewitnesses to keep their anti-supernatural worldview intact. No amount of evidence which you will present will convince someone who does not like the implications of the evidence:

> This is true of even the most "convincing" Christian argument—a cogent case for the historicity of the resurrection. Upon hearing such an argument, one listener may reply, "Aha, this *is* ultimately a chance universe in which even the most unexpected of things can happen once. A man rising from the dead, can you imagine that?" Or another may say, "Erik Von Daniken must be right. Jesus must have been one of those men from outer space, evidently from a planet where men are so constituted that they come back to life after dying." In neither case has the data been

seen to confirm that claim which it was intended to confirm—that Jesus is divine, the Son of God.[10]

How can this be? Why doesn't evidence always convince? In the case of evidence relating to Jesus Christ, once a person acknowledges that Jesus is indeed the Son of God, then a change of life is in order. Repentance from sin and trusting in His finished work on the cross is the necessary response in light of the evidence. In order to avoid submission to Christ, many people are willing to dismiss the facts or reinterpret them to be absolved of having to face the risen Christ. The naturalist must find ways to explain away the apparently *super*natural; when an explanation is not readily available, he asks for more time—rather than abandoning his naturalism as a philosophy.

4. Worldviews are Exclusive

The Christian worldview cannot exist in the same arena of thought with contrary worldviews at the same time. Non-Christian worldviews often work together to displace the Christian worldview. Of course, the Christian worldview should be working to displace the non-Christian worldviews. In principle, there is never any room for compromise. (In practice, however, both a believer and an unbeliever can work together to stop abortion, help the poor, or build a hospital. Why? The unbeliever is working within the Christian's worldview.) Communism's goal, for example, is to eradicate any vestige of God from the universe.

> The Communist vision is the vision of Man without God. It is the vision of man's mind displacing God as the creative intelligence of the world. It is the vision of man's liberated mind, by the sole force of his rational intelligence, redirecting man's destiny and reorganizing man's life and the world. It is the vision of man, once more the central figure of the Creation, not because God made man in His image, but because man's mind makes him the most intelligent of the animals. Copernicus and his successors displaced man as the central fact of the universe by proving that the earth was not the central star of the universe. Communism restores man to his sovereignty by the simple method of denying God.[11]

Non-Christian belief systems cannot afford to allow competition. As long as people believe in a higher law or another sovereign, then the new ideology can never completely win over the people.

WAR OF THE WORLDVIEWS

Nazism is a classic expression of the exclusive nature of worldviews. Nazi Germany brings to mind the extermination of the Jews in what has been called the Holocaust. Adolf Hitler's disenfranchisement of the Jews in Germany in the 1930s and 1940s is a prominent theme in any study of World War II, Germany, or political tyranny. The Jews were slowly and efficiently barred from economic, educational, and political participation. Eventually they were driven from the nation. What many people do not know is that the Christian church was put on notice to either follow the Nazi Party line or be closed down. William Shirer, author of *The Rise and Fall of the Third Reich*, writes that under the leadership of Alfred Rosenberg, an outspoken pagan, "the Nazi regime intended eventually to destroy Christianity in Germany, if it could, and substitute the old paganism of the early tribal Germanic gods and the new paganism of the Nazi extremists. As Bormann, one of the men closest to Hitler, said publicly in 1941, 'National Socialism and Christianity are irreconcilable.'"[12] Shirer in *The Nightmare Years*, writes: "We know now what Hitler envisioned for the German Christians: the utter suppression of their religion."[13] The internal intelligence agency of the Nazi SS "regarded organized Christianity as one of the major obstacles to the establishment of a truly totalitarian state."[14] Why? Christians believe that there is another King, Jesus (Acts 17:7).

In *Mein Kampf* Hitler stressed "the importance of winning over and then training the youth in the service 'of a new national state.'"[15] Shirer continues by showing how Hitler used education as a device to direct the future of the nation:

> "When an opponent declares, 'I will not come over to your side,'" he said in a speech on November 6, 1933, "I calmly say, 'Your child belongs to us already, . . . What are you? You will pass on. Your descendants, however, now stand in the new camp. In a short time they will know nothing else but this new community.'"
> And on May 1, 1937, he declared, "This new Reich will give its youth to no one, but will itself take youth and give to youth its own education and its own upbringing."[16]

All the German schools "were quickly Nazified." Control was taken away from the parents and local authorities and "[e]very person in the teaching profession, from kindergarten through the universities, was compelled to join the National Socialist Teachers' League which, by law, was held 'responsible for the execution of the ideological and political coordination of all the teachers in accordance with the National Socialist doctrine.'"[17] Only the Nazi worldview was permitted.

Of course, this is an extreme example. But our nation's public schools are bastions of intolerance. In Greenville, Tennessee, some Christian parents wanted alternative textbooks for their children. Here's what a syndicated columnist had to say about the incident:

> These poor children are being denied the most basic of childhood's freedoms, the right to imagine and learn. Someone should remind their parents the law of this land still requires we educate our children in qualified schools with qualified teachers. That a sound education involves free exploration of ideas and fact. That they may rant and rave against humanism and feminism and any other "ism" on Sunday, but come Monday the children belong in school.[18]

The Christian worldview is relegated to the church. You can have your religious views but keep them private. According to a recent radio editorial, "a man's religion and the strength of his conviction are his own personal matter. Religion should not interfere with politics."[19] I wonder what he would say about the abolition of the slave trade in England and the civil rights movement in the United States? These movements were headed by religious leaders who were motivated out of religious conviction.

5. Worldviews are Transformational

Worldviews are seen as vehicles for cultural transformation. Many in the entertainment field, for example, believe that they are the nation's conscience and the only guiding light. In an interview with film director and producer Francis Ford Coppola, the aggressive nature and comprehensive effects of worldviews come to light:

> My dream is that the artist class—people who have proven through their work that they are humanists and wish to push for what Aldous Huxley called the desirable human potentialities of intelligence, creativity and friendliness—will seize the instrument of technology and try to take humanity into a period of history in which we can reach for a utopia. Of course, it is possible for the technology to be misused—we could end up with a Big Brother—but we could also have a balanced society, with an

artist class leading the culture toward something approximating a happy family or tribe.

At the moment, the nation is in a fog, and we've got to put our headlights on. Artists—those who rely on their intuition—can be the nation's headlights.[20]

Coppola believes that an "artist class" is the only group that can establish a consistent and workable worldview. But he goes even further. He wants us to believe that an artist class should be in the position of worldview leadership. Apparently, no other group or combination of groups is capable of articulating a worldview without their innate expertise. An artist's "intuition" is the basic presupposed authority for Coppola. Nearly every discipline maintains the same exclusivity. We could substitute "lawyer class," "economic class," "education class," "science class," or "medical class" for "artist class."

THE RADICALIZATION PROCESS

The college setting is a perfect example of how secularists must break down traditional beliefs. In other words, professors want to "radicalize" their students so that they will adopt a secularized, man-centered, naturalistic worldview. New facts are presented to force students to give up their presuppositions. Their techniques are similar to indoctrination and brainwashing methods used by the Chinese Communists. The following is written by a professor who understands the necessity of a solid worldview based on firm convictions. His worldview is radically opposed to a Biblical worldview; therefore, his advice is valuable. Through his words you will understand how the skeptic thinks:

> Your feelings of insecurity may be greatly increased by our ruthlessly ripping away the myths which have supported your faith in yourself and America. This faith has been one of the basic sources of security, and learning the truth about the Pilgrims, the Indians, and the Philippines, and so on can make you feel terribly alone and insecure.
>
> The social necessities for telling you the truth have already been discussed, but you should also realize that the truth may hurt, but you can be secure without it—one prick of the truth and you'll explode. The Chinese Communists proved that by using

selective versions of American history as a brainwashing technique. They told American prisoners part of the truth about our history, and the men just folded up.

However, the Chinese Communists also realized that this technique would not work on people with a solid understanding of the truth. They therefore *didn't even try* to brainwash most officers and college-educated men. The experiences in the Korean prisoners-of-war camps are one of the most dramatic illustrations of a principle we college professors never tire of pointing out: *knowledge, real knowledge, not myths, or propaganda, is the firmest and surest foundation for psychological security.*[21]

You would like to believe that college is the place where more facts are added to an already growing reservoir of knowledge, and that higher education merely teaches students a greater understanding of the real world. To a certain extent, college students will gain a better understanding of the world. But at the same time a great deal of propaganda and indoctrination will accompany the facts. Universities want to give students the impression that professors are simply men and women who have a neutral grasp of the facts. Allegedly, they are not filtering the facts through any preconceived worldview. Why, they wouldn't be teaching at the university level unless they really knew the impartial, unbiased truth. This is what they want you to believe. The sad thing is that most professors believe this, and many students fall for it.

This is not a true portrait of college life. In fact, life in general does not operate like this. Some philosophy of life always guides a person, and tensions develop because of competition between competing philosophies or worldviews. The worldview which is most subject to attack is the Christian worldview because it maintains that no claim to truth (factuality) is neutral. Non-Christians believe in a philosophical "pluralism" where all worldviews must be considered valid except any worldview which insists that its way is the only way. The Christian realizes that portrayals of reality are interpreted "reality." Everybody has primary commitments (not based on observation) that he uses to organize and interpret the facts. Therefore all worldviews, if their starting points differ, are at war with one another. And all non-Christian worldviews are together at war with the Christian worldview.

Regulating Reality

The facts that support a position are chosen and interpreted in terms of religiously held presuppositions. Apparent "facts" that do not fit the presuppositions may be discarded as non-facts. At times, people recognize that there are many, many facts that cannot fit into their interpretive framework. Sometimes, an investigation of these facts will lead the person to change a previous opinion. In many cases, though, the facts that don't fit are thrown out. Certain facts must be omitted because of a commitment to an opposing worldview.

Secularists will tell you that man is the "determiner of all things"; a woman has a right to do what she wants with her own body; those in political control can use the power of the State to "create" a "just" society; all sexual choices are proper and good choices, etc. Relativism is a religious law that regulates interpretation of all facts. It's a religious declaration, and it gives meaning to everything else someone says. If a person is an evolutionist, then he will see things in terms of an evolutionary worldview.

Starting with atheism to evaluate the world demands that all the facts be squeezed through this anti-theistic grid. If a study of the design of the human body seems to demonstrate the necessity of a designer, then that fact must either be discarded as a non-fact, and therefore never considered for discussion, or the design of an organism must be interpreted in terms of a non-theistic conception of reality. For example, "the *wisdom* of DNA." In other words, "Nature" might be personified to take the place of a personal God. The random choices of Nature brought about design. Of course, it is rarely explained how this could be. Just as it's never explained how matter came into existence in the first place. What, after all, "caused" the universe to come into existence so that we even have "Nature"?

What exactly is "Nature" except a summary expression for the way things happen. In that case, "Nature" does not explain the way things happen. But atheists prefer empty references to "Nature" over guilt-inducing references to a Creator God who judges man in his sin.

There can be no room in the atheist's world for any fact that might point to a Creator, a God who stands over man in judgment and evaluation. Any evidence that seems to point to a Creator somehow must be explained away or ignored.

WORLDVIEWS IN CONFLICT

A LITTLE LOWER THAN THE ANGELS

What determines how we think and act? Are our actions nothing more than a series of chemical reactions and nerve responses? Should man be defined solely in terms of his biochemical makeup or is there more to us than meets the eye? For some modern thinkers, science has redefined man, not in terms of special creation, but in terms of biology:

> [The] sciences owe their spectacular progress to the assumption that all the processes of life can be interpreted finally as simply physical and chemical ones. Many of them have been imitated in the laboratory test-tube. The actions of enzymes, hormones, nucleic acids, complex proteins, and other substances concerned with the processes of life in general, so far as science can analyze them, follow the same laws that govern all the lifeless universe. To many the conclusion is now obvious that man, like every other living thing, is only a material mechanism, extraordinarily complex but no different in his basic nature from any other piece of machinery. This conception readily solves the dilemma of man's dual nature by denying that the intangible mental and spiritual side of him really exists at all.[22]

We are all religious beings with a spiritual nature. We are created this way. Biology does not make us unique. The scientist will not find the human spirit under a microscope. Man as a biological unit means we are nothing more than "naked apes." Describing man in mechanistic terms will transform humanity into an organic machine. Consider what can happen to man when he is no longer afforded the dignity of previous generations. What's to stop the powerful from using the weak for their own unjust ends? Totalitarian regimes around the world are noted for their inhumanity to man. Why should man be treated in any way different from the animals when the belief prevails that man is nothing more than a highly complex evolving animal? Why not experiment on man to see what makes him tick? Maybe we can accelerate the process of evolution and create supermen.

> With the philosophy of modern science, what is to stop genetic transfers of animal genes into humans? There is no secular ethic that can effectively argue against such things. Once the concept of man's uniqueness as being created in the image of God is lost, then all logical defenses against fusing man and animal are, at

best, spurious. This obviously calls into question the worth of human beings in the man-animal-machine complex once the distinctions are blurred.[23]

In time man will rebel against this dehumanization. Man is more than ape, more than a mechanism. We cannot escape this fact, although there are many who want us to try. But to deny our spiritual nature is to deny what makes us uniquely human. All that we hold valuable, good, and true are lost when men deny their essential spiritual nature. The loss of a Biblical view of man where God is sovereign over all the affairs of men tends to elevate some other sovereign to the place of God. In the classroom, this is usually the "expert." In society, this usually means the State. When a civil government adopts the view that man is less than what the Bible says, you can expect the dignity of man to be stripped from him. "Historically Western society has derived its belief in the dignity of man from its Judeo-Christian belief that man is the glory of God, made in His image. According to this view, human rights depend upon the creator who made man with dignity, not upon the state. In the American formulation, 'men . . . are endowed by their creator with certain inalienable rights.' "[24]

CONCLUSION

In the twentieth century, Biblical Christianity has fallen on hard times. This is so not because of any legitimacy inherent in secular worldviews. Rather, the Christian worldview has not been well articulated. In fact, many Christians have seen no need to apply the Bible beyond the limits of personal salvation and the life to come. In a word, the Bible has little or nothing to say to this world. Modern culture, therefore, has adopted other worldviews to replace the once-prevailing worldview of Biblical Christianity. The results have been less than encouraging.

> In the past sixty years there has been more brutality and obscurantism, more senseless conflicts, more of the past's heritage destroyed, more crass idolatry, more lies and hoaxes perpetuated, more people murdered or cast adrift as undesirable elements than in any other time in history; most of this in purportedly just causes for the advancement of mankind in general.[25]

When the former darling of the media, Aleksandr Solzhenitsyn, said, "Man has forgotten God, that is why this has happened," the intelligentsia aimed "their barbs of 'simplistic' at the author of *The Gulag Archipelago*."[26] But it is that simple.

WORLDVIEWS IN CONFLICT

When man forgets God, he adopts some other principle and makes it the god of his life. The god of modern political states, for example, is power. In the Bible, when man rejected God as his Sovereign Ruler, tyrants with promises of salvation were always eager to fill in as the new political deity. But with the promise of salvation also came the reality of tyranny.

> And the bramble said to the trees, "If in truth you are anointing me as king over you, come and take refuge in my shade; but if not, may fire come out from the bramble and consume the cedars of Lebanon" (Judges 9:15).

Even after God warned the Israelites what it would mean to reject Him, the people still chose a tyrant to rule over them (1 Samuel 8).

Times have not changed. On May 28th, 1849, Robert C. Winthrop addressed the Annual Meeting of the Massachusetts Bible Society in Boston. He made it clear that "ideas have consequences," especially ideas that remove God from the equation of life.

> All societies of men must be governed in some way or other. The less they may have of stringent State Government, the more they must have of individual self-government. The less they rely on public law or physical force, the more they must rely on private moral restraint. Men, in a word, must necessarily be controlled, either by a power within them, or by a power without them; either by the Word of God, or by the strong arm of man; either by the Bible, or by the bayonet. It may do for other countries and other governments to talk about the State supporting religion. Here, under our own free institutions, it is Religion which must support the State.

The bayonet rules in those nations which reject Jesus Christ and His Word. As the Bible ceases to govern in the hearts of the people, and those who rule reject the Bible as a standard of righteousness, we will see more of the glistening steel of the sharpened bayonet ruling in America and around the world.

3
THE CHRISTIAN WORLDVIEW

> Just as old or bleary-eyed men and those with weak vision, if you thrust before them a most beautiful volume, even if they recognize it to be some sort of writing, yet can scarcely construe two words, but with the aid of spectacles will begin to read distinctly; so Scripture, gathering up the otherwise confused knowledge of God in our minds, having dispersed our dullness, clearly shows us the true God.[1]

WHAT makes up the Christian worldview? The foundation of a proper study of God, the universe, and man is God and His revelation, not man and his ideas about God. God gives meaning to the universe and to man. Now, there are all types of descriptions of "God": from Aristotle's Prime Mover to Shirley MacLaine's belief that God is a part of all of us and we are a part of God. Our description of God, therefore, must go beyond the mere belief in *a* god; we must consider the one *true* God. Our foundation then is the God of the Bible, because it is in Scripture that God reveals Himself. All other descriptions of God must be evaluated in terms of the Bible's witness.

1. *God is the Creator.* While the universe had a beginning, the God of the Bible is eternally self-existent in three Persons—Father, Son, and Holy Spirit. God made the created order, what is commonly referred to as "Nature," out of nothing. This is called creation *ex nihilo*. This doctrine is unique to Christianity. God did not create out of His own being (*ex deo*) or out of pre-existing material (*ex materia*).

2. *God is Personal and Triune.* God is not a "thing" like a tree or a "force" like electricity. He is a person. One question about the creation

of man that a child often asks is, Why did God create man? Many parents have given this simple answer: Because He was lonely. But this is not what the Bible teaches. The Persons of the Godhead—what the Church has called "the Trinity"[2]—communicated with one another before man was created. They could communicate because they are persons. Each Person of the Godhead thinks, wills, and acts, never in opposition, always in unity. Since communication takes place between the Persons of the Godhead, as creatures created in the image of this Triune God, we too can communicate with Him and with one another.

3. *God is both Lord and Father.* In many pagan worldview philosophies, the gods are either so exalted, transcendent, and "otherly" that they do not identify with men, or they are so much like men that they are unpredictable and at times helpless and even sinful. The Bible describes God as Lord and Father, two terms that express God's transcendence and immanence.*

> *_Immanence_ is the quality of being near at hand or involved in man's temporal experience.

As our Lord, God is sovereign, ruler, and teacher. He is mighty, mysterious, exalted, and powerful so that He's able to do all things. As our Father, God is tender in mercy, compassionate, loving, patient, forgiving, and always willing to listen even to our most feeble prayers. He meets with us in our creaturehood and identifies with us in our weakness. Yet, these two ways of looking at God are not mutually exclusive. The transcendence (God is *distinct from* us) and immanence (God is *near to* us) of God are not contradictory concepts. John Frame writes:

> These two attributes do not conflict with one another. God is close *because* he is Lord. He is Lord, and thus free to make his power felt everywhere we go. He is Lord, and thus able to reveal himself clearly to us, distinguishing himself from all mere creatures. He is Lord, and therefore the most central fact of our experience, the least avoidable, the most verifiable.[3]

God can be our Father because He is our Lord. Because God is all-powerful, He can do what He pleases. He can help us. God has chosen to love rebellious sinners who want nothing of His love. Because He is the all-powerful Lord of all things, He can love those who do not deserve to be loved. What non-Christian worldview has this to offer you?

4. *God knows everything.* God knows intuitively. He does not have to search for more information to make a decision. All the knowledge in the universe is at His disposal. His knowledge makes the universe what it is. There is no new knowledge for God. God's thoughts are thus "original" and "independent." While ours are always "derivative" and "dependent." This means that God can never be mistaken about anything; therefore, what God tells us is true. If there is any misunderstanding or misapplication of God's Word, the fault lies with us. God has not chosen to reveal to us all that He knows. Much of what God knows is described as "secret things" (Deuteronomy 29:29). But He has revealed to us all we need to know.

5. *God is good, holy, and just.* One of the first attributes that a child learns about God is that He is good. God's goodness tells us what God *is* and how He *acts*. Goodness is not above God as an abstract idea. *God is goodness*, and He always acts in terms of His goodness. This means that He cares for all of His creation, from the plants and animals to men and women, even rebellious men and women. But God's goodness is not cheap and sentimental, because God is also holy. "Who is like Thee among the gods, O LORD? Who is like Thee, majestic in holiness, awesome in praises, working wonders?" (Exodus 15:11). The holiness of God is one of the most awesome themes in the Bible. Holiness has a very rich meaning in Scripture, but part of God's holiness is His perfect sinlessness. He is light, and there is no darkness in Him. To be in the presence of a thrice-holy God is disturbing, especially to rebel sinners. Isaiah described it as being "ruined" (Isaiah 6:5).

God's justice is the working out of His holy nature and will. This means that there are ethical absolutes that have God's character as their reference point. God's "work is perfect, for all His ways are just; a God of faithfulness and without injustice, righteousness and upright is He" (Deuteronomy 32:4). God's law then is a reflection of God's perfect character of holiness, goodness, and justice. There can be no ethical relativism in God or in His law.

Created in God's Image

God personalized His creation by creating man in His own image. This means that man reflects the attributes of God in a way that no other creature does. Animals have not been created in God's image. Man has a personality because God has a personality. Man is rational because God is rational. Man is self-conscious because God is self-conscious; that is, man can think about and judge himself. But there remains a fundamental Creator/creature distinction. Man does not possess these and other attributes of God in the same degree as God possesses them. For example, while God knows everything, as creatures we know only some things, and what we do know, we do not know in a comprehensive way. What we do know, however, we know truly. While we might not understand all the implications of what the Bible means when it says that God created the world out of nothing, we do know something of what is involved in that assertion. The idealist philosophers imply that knowledge is impossible until *all* the facts are known. The Creator/creature distinction means that we will never become more than creatures. We will not evolve into gods or even angels.

There is a fundamental distinction between God's being and man's being. First, God is uncreated (self-existent), independent, infinite, eternal, and unchangeable, while man is created (derivative), dependent, finite, temporal, and changeable. What does this mean in practical terms? When the creature denies God, he works to take on God's attributes for himself. But if every man decides that he is god in an absolute sense, we end up with moral anarchy. So, what happens? Some *institution* takes on the divine attributes, usually civil government, the State. The State then acts as if it were god—a tyrannical and capricious god: controlling lives, confiscating property, closing the borders of the country in order to keep its "subjects" from going to what the State perceives to be another god, and imprisoning those who defy the new god-State. Conde Pallen's utopian novel depicts what happens when the true God is rejected. Man looks for a suitable substitute:

> *Q.* By whom were you begotten?
> *A.* By the sovereign State.
> *Q.* Why were you begotten?
> *A.* That I might know, love, and serve the Sovereign State always.
> *Q.* What is the sovereign State?
> *A.* The sovereign State is humanity in composite and perfect being.
> *Q.* Why is the State supreme?
> *A.* The State is supreme because it is my Creator and Conserver in which I am and move and have my being and without which I am nothing.

Q. What is the individual?
A. The individual is only a part of the whole, and made for the whole, and finds his complete and perfect expression in the sovereign State. Individuals are made for cooperation only, like feet, like hands, like eyelids, like the rows of the upper and lower teeth.[4]

He Is There and He Is Not Silent[5]

One of the most controversial doctrines of the Christian worldview is the belief that God can and does reveal Himself so men can really know Him: First, in general revelation; second, in written, special revelation; and third, in the Person of Jesus Christ.

In general revelation God speaks to man through the created order. "The heavens are telling of the glory of God; and their expanse is declaring the works of His hands. Day to day pours forth speech. And night to night reveals knowledge" (Psalm 19:1-2). If the creation could speak as a man, it would pour forth words day in and day out that God is the one who created the world. The creation is His handiwork. This is why the Apostle Paul could write of how inexcusable it is to deny God when you look at the created order. "For since the creation of the world His invisible attributes, His eternal power and divine nature, have been clearly seen, being understood through what has been made, *so they are without excuse*" (Romans 1:20). Something has to account for what exists. The humanist opts for evolution: time, plus chance, plus pre-existent and impersonal matter.

While general revelation tells us that God exists, it also shows us what kind of God exists. Romans 1:21 says unbelievers know "*the* God." They *know* "what kind" of God He is through

- His invisible attributes (v. 20).
- His everlasting power (v. 20).
- His divine status (v. 20).
- His deserving of thanks (v. 21).
- His glory (v. 23).
- His moral character (vv. 24-32).

They know so much that they are "completely without excuse" for their pagan ideas and behavior (v. 20). They "suppress the truth" (v. 18).

Although we can learn from the created order that God is powerful and glorious, general revelation does not reveal *everything* we need to know about God. So God has not left us without a *special* revelation of Himself. Special revelation comes to man in four ways: (1) in displays of power (the pillar of fire and the cloud of smoke that accompanied Israel in the wilderness); (2) specific one-time appearances (to Moses at the burning bush); (3) direct verbal communication (to prophets); (4) written, propositional revelation (as in the Bible). These types of revelation are called "special" because they are outside the normal workings of creation or general revelation. In each of the four methods of communication, God enters history to communicate directly with His people.

Of course, God went even beyond this by becoming man and entering history in the Person of Jesus Christ. Jesus' words were the very words of God. We have many of them recorded in the Bible, our only depository of God's revelation. The significant point here is that the Biblical worldview maintains that God can and does clearly communicate with man. This means that we can know God intimately. We can know who and what He is, and we can know His will. No other philosophy of life can make such a claim. This is why Christianity is exclusive. All other supposed revelations must be judged by God's special revelation, the Bible.

Man Lives in the Midst of a Fallen World

Not only must a worldview explain why something exists; it must also explain why it exists the *way* it does. God created the world and proclaimed it to be "very good" (Genesis 1:31). God's standards of righteousness were exhibited in the created order. There was neither death nor decay. But man chose to ignore God's commands and decided to live by his own rules. After the Fall, the world could no longer be described as "very good." Adam and Eve were cast out of paradise, and entered a world where the ground brought forth thorns and thistles (Genesis 3:18). Adam and Eve's rebellion brought about death, not only in the created order but for man himself:

> In *personality*, man lost his capacity to know himself accurately and to determine his own course of action freely in response to his intelligence. His *self-transcendence* was impaired by the alienation he experienced in relation to God, for as man turned from God, God let him go. And as man slipped from close fellowship with the ultimately transcendent one, so he lost his ability to

stand over against the external universe, understand it, judge it accurately and thus make truly "free" decisions. Rather, he became more a servant to nature than to God. And his status as God's vice-regent over nature (an aspect of the image of God) was reversed.

Man's *intelligence* also became impaired. Now he can no longer gain a fully accurate knowledge of the world around him, nor is he able to reason without constantly falling into error. *Morally*, man became less able to discern good and evil. *Socially*, he began to exploit his fellow men. *Creatively*, his imagination became separated from reality; imagination became illusion, and artists who created gods in their own image led man further and further from their origin. The vacuum in man created by this string of consequences is ominous indeed. (The fullest Biblical expression of these ideas is Romans 1-2).

Theologians have summed it up this way: Man has become alienated from God, from others, from nature and even from himself. This is the essence of man *fallen*.[6]

This explains why the world is in a mess. Man is not a mere product of his environment. Man has turned against God, and in turn, against other men, himself, and his world. Man's rebellion has twisted the created order and man; they can no longer be described as "very good." Only the Bible can adequately explain injustice, poverty, death, war, famine, and man's inhumanity toward other men.

Only in the Biblical worldview is there any hope of change, any chance of redemption. The Bible tells us why the world is in a mess, and the Bible shows us how to clean it up. This brings us back to the special revelation of the Lord Jesus Christ. Through His perfect life and His redeeming work, man can be changed; the image of God can be restored. "Man *redeemed* is man on the way to restoration of the defaced image—in other words, substantial healing in every area—personality, self-transcendence, intelligence, morality, social capacity and creativity."[7] And if man can be changed, so can the world. Even in death, there is hope. The Bible shows in vivid terms what lies beyond the grave. Only in Christ is the sting of death removed. No other worldview can offer such comfort and assurance.

THE DOMINO EFFECT OF DISBELIEF

You might have seen the TV show that aired a number of years ago called "That's Incredible," in which the good, the bad, and the unusual were paraded before the television viewing audience each week. One of the most ingenious feats ever performed was a world record domino extravaganza. Thousands of dominos were placed in intricate designs on a gymnasium floor by a "domino technician" who had to be careful not to allow even one domino to fall prematurely. The fall of the first domino would bring the entire exhibition to a less than incredible climax.

Ideas, like those dominos, are interdependent. If the first domino in a worldview begins to fall, you can expect the rest to follow eventually. The Christian worldview begins with the belief in a personal God who created and upholds all things. But the Christian worldview does not stop with creation and providence. God communicates with those whom He created in His own image through a written revelation that has come to be called the Bible. But what if one of these essential beliefs is denied? Can we expect that in time they all might be denied? Deny a personal God, and man becomes his own god. Deny that a personal God created and now sustains the universe, and you end up with a chance universe where anything is possible. Deny the reality of a written revelation, and all truth seems to be relative. Such denials set off a series of dominos of unbelief.

Domino One: Deism

Deism is the weakened bridge between Biblical Christianity and naturalism. In Biblical Christianity, the universe is dependent on God for its existence as well as its maintenance. These are the doctrines of *creation* and *providence*. In deism the Biblical doctrine of providence is denied. The Bible says that God *"upholds all things* by the word of His power" (Hebrews 1:3). The worldview of deism proposes that a *"transcendent God, as a First Cause, created the universe but then left it to run on its own. God is thus not immanent, not fully personal, not sovereign over the affairs of men, not providential."*[8] The Christian worldview is therefore opposed to deism. While deism is formally "theistic," it is not Biblical; it does not have a doctrine of providence.

Deism was a prominent and self-conscious worldview during the post-revolutionary war period. Some of our nation's most famous founders have been classified as deists.[9] While deism is not an articulated worldview, today many religious people subscribe to it unknowingly. For them, God exists, but He does not concern Himself intimately with His creation. Some go so far as to maintain that God is powerless to work in the world. The reason bad things happen to good people, (as the book by a similar name insists), is that God is unable to intervene in people's lives or the affairs of this world. God is finite and thus unable to alleviate the suffering of men and women.

As you can probably tell, it is not very difficult for the first domino of the Christian worldview to fall with the presuppositions of deism. Deism maintains a transcendent God and a created universe. But it also postulates a God who is virtually impotent, and a worldview of "Nature" that has assumed His power. A person can be very religious and still be a deist. But once someone accepts the presuppositions of deism, he is ripe for the worldview of naturalism.

Domino Two: Naturalism

The next domino to fall is the presupposition that there is nothing more than the observable world or the world of man's temporal experience. Even naturalists insist that we have experiences that are not of "observable" things. Magnetic fields? God is put outside the world in deism. In naturalism, God is banished from the universe altogether, either as a force or as an explanation. We live in a world in which the Spiritual dimension of reality has been expunged from the universe. Carl Sagan of *Cosmos* fame expressed the fundamental presupposition of naturalism well: "The Cosmos is all that is or ever was or ever will be."[10] But of course Sagan did not *observe* that the Cosmos is all there is! It is his faith assumption. Science is inherently unable to tell us its own limits. All of life must be explained in terms of what can be observed and scientifically tested. There is no Spiritual dimension to the universe. Naturalism is Flatland country.

> In 1884 Edwin Abbot published the story of "Flatland." Flatland is an imaginary country where everyone lives in only two dimensions. The people are circles, triangles and squares, and they live in pentagons. A line to them is like a wall to us. They do not know up or down, only north, south, east and west.
>
> One day a sphere came to visit Flatland. At first the Flatlanders could not see him because the sphere remained outside their

plane. They were confused by a voice that was not associated with a line, and they did not understand when he told them that he was "above" them. . . . So the sphere entered Flatland. Of course, to the Flatlanders he appeared to be a circle. But he talked to them about a three-dimensional world that was beyond their experiences.[11]

For the most part, contemporary culture is Flatland country. Biblical revelation remains outside the plane of those who believe as Carl Sagan believes. Their presuppositions cannot accommodate God, and if God were ever to enter history personally, as He did in the person of Jesus Christ, or propositionally as He speaks to man in the Bible, there would be no way for a Flatlander to recognize Him. A Flatlander's explanation would go something like this: There are no spheres (God speaking to man in special revelation), only circles (the world that we see around us and nothing more). A three-dimensional world is inconceivable and therefore can never be observed.

The tests that would be given to certify the claims of a personal God entering history or a written revelation that is God's very word would not be adequate to measure them. The surveyors would continue to come up with circles instead of spheres. Their naturalistic presuppositions would get in the way of the actual facts. The idea of a personal God entering history would be only the imaginary aspirations of a Flatlander who wanted to escape a two-dimensional world for a three-dimensional world that does not exist. Special revelation would be nothing more than the writings of some Flatlanders that simply *depicted* a fictional three-dimensional world. That three-dimensional world certainly does not exist.

Naturalism* teaches that nature is the whole of reality. The worldview of naturalism shuts man inside a closed universe. Naturalism is similar to the worldview of those who believed in a flat earth. Explorers were afraid to sail to the "ends" of the earth. Their false worldview limited their knowledge.

Naturalism as a philosophical worldview should not be confused with "naturalism" as a study of wildlife.

Since what is studied by the techniques of natural science is all that there is, there is no need for exploration that goes beyond the universe.

THE CHRISTIAN WORLDVIEW

Nature is defined in terms of the material realm, broadly defined. The universe has its "origin" in pre-existent matter and thus has no real existence apart from it; therefore, the universe cannot be explained in any other terms. There is no "mind," for example. Thought is reduced to the chemical processes of brain tissue. Values are culturally determined and are therefore always in flux. Religion and the idea of God are the projections of people who want to believe in something beyond what they can see. A worldview that is synonymous with naturalism is secular* humanism.

> *Secular* comes from the Latin *saeculum*, which means "time" or "age." Today, to describe someone as secular means he is completely bound to time with no vision of eternity. This means when you are dead, you are dead. Nothing is beyond the grave since man is nothing more than a complex combination of matter. Man has no Spiritual dimension. Of course, this also means that matter is eternal. Nothing existed before matter, certainly not a god. The secularist cannot and will not believe that God exists or acts in human affairs.

The following proposition is fundamental to the naturalistic or secular system of thought:

> As non-theists, we begin with humans, not God, nature not deity. Nature may indeed be broader and deeper than we now know; and new discoveries, however, will but enlarge our knowledge of the natural.[12]

What presuppositions make up the worldview of naturalism?

1. *The universe is self-existent.* There can be no other explanation for what exists. The universe either came into existence out of nothing (the Christian position), or the universe in some form always existed.

2. *The universe consists solely of matter.* Since there is no personal God beyond the universe who controls the universe, then matter is all there is. There is no "spirit" or "soul" that can reside in man.

3. *The universe is evolving.* What we see today may not be here tomorrow. Chance dictates the direction the universe will take. In fact, man may not be the highest of evolved animals in another million years. *The Planet of the Apes* is a real possibility with naturalism.

4. *Man is nothing more than a highly evolved animal.* Man is nothing more than a reflection of the universe. He is the universe in microcosm; therefore, he can have no "soul" or "mind." (When naturalists speak as if man has a mind or can make free choices, they are being inconsistent with their worldview. Man is not greater than his "creator.")

5. *The end of man is extinction.* There is no God. There can be no judgment, no heaven, no hell. Life after death, while it may be a possibility, is still left to chance and ignorance. No one can know with naturalism. (The best naturalism can offer is extinction and scant reports of "bright lights" as people near death's door and soon return with stories of "peacefulness" and "tranquility." With naturalism, why does it matter? Man is nothing more than matter: simply a conglomeration of atoms.)

6. *There can be no certainty.* The naturalist can never be certain that what he believes is true. Given the fact (as naturalism teaches) that everything is evolving, "truth" itself must be in flux. What is "true" today may be "false" tomorrow. "One could well ask: 'If the mind, like all else in nature, is still evolving, how can we be sure that its present structure and operation guarantee any truth?' For example, did the Law of Contradiction, which is necessary for truth, evolve like the rest of the body? How can we be sure that there's not some new mental law, now struggling to be born, a law which will enable us to get even closer to the truth about reality? Would this new law confirm or contradict evolution and naturalism?"[13] With naturalism, we would never know. Charles Darwin understood the implications of his own evolutionary theory: "With me the horrid doubt always arises whether the convictions of man's mind, which has been developed from the mind of the lower animals, are of any value or at all trustworthy. Would anyone trust in the convictions of a monkey's mind, if there are any convictions in such a mind?"[14]

7. *Naturalism is committed to miracles.* The naturalist would have us believe that: "Everything came from nothing. Order came from chaos. Harmony came from discord. Life came from nonlife. Reason came from irrationality. Personality came from nonpersonality. Morality came from amorality."[15]

8. *History has no purpose.* Why should the naturalist expect history to "go anywhere" or to "mean" anything? The naturalist cannot predict future events based on past events, because there is no regularity in history. Henry Ford's words that "history is more or less bunk" becomes a truism while George Santayana's dictum that "those who cannot remember the past are condemned to repeat it" turns into nonsense.

THE CHRISTIAN WORLDVIEW

9. *Man's purpose in life is self-actualization, hedonism, and narcissism.* Pleasure may often be the only goal of the naturalist, since for him man is nothing more than an animal. Sense perceptions are the only important considerations. The "good" is relative to the time, place, and tastes of particular persons. The pain of others can be "self-actualizing" for some hedonists. A Marquis de Sade is at home with a naturalistic worldview. For the naturalist it is "Let us eat and drink, for tomorrow we may die" (Isaiah 22:13). The Apostle links a belief in the resurrection with this verse: "If the dead are not raised, 'Let us eat and drink, for tomorrow we die'" (1 Corinthians 15:32).

10. *Man "saves" himself through education, law, science, technology, and politics.* One of the doctrinal pillars of the *Humanist Manifesto II* is, "No deity will save us; we must save ourselves."[16] And how does the naturalist propose that man will save us?: "Using technology wisely, we can control our environment, conquer poverty, markedly reduce disease, extend our life-span, significantly modify our behavior, alter the course of human evolution and cultural development, unlock vast new powers, and provide humankind with unparalleled opportunity for achieving an abundant and meaningful life."[17]

11. *Values are relative and subjective.* What type of ethical norms should we expect from a self-existent universe, an evolving order, and a biological component called man? Values evolve along with man and his world. Ethical considerations are tied to whatever works for maximizing the pleasure of the greatest number. (But then why is *that* ethically obligatory?) Joseph Fletcher sums up this avenue of the naturalistic worldview on ethics with this declaration: "I think there are no normative moral principles whatsoever which are intrinsically valid or universally obliging."[18]

12. *Human life is expendable.* We kill animals for food. Man is only a highly evolved animal. Therefore man can be killed for any number of "socially acceptable reasons": over-population, high medical costs for the terminally ill, and the inconveniences of too many children. After a debate on the abortion issue, a lawyer who had participated in the debate had the opportunity to speak with some of the other participants: "[M]ost of the students *already* recognized that the unborn child is a human life. Nevertheless, certain social reasons are considered 'high enough' to justify ending that life. According to some of the women, examples of 'high enough' reasons include protecting pregnant teenagers from the psychological distress of bearing a child, helping poor women who aren't able to care adequately for a child, and preventing children

from coming into the world 'unwanted.' Many charged that pro-life philosophies are not 'socially acceptable' because they fail to deal realistically with these problems."[19]

13. *All lifestyles are permissible while the family is considered obsolete.* Once ethical norms become arbitrary, we can expect the dismantling of long-standing Christian familial relationships like marriage and heterosexuality. Social relationships have to evolve along with nature. For example, in Marxist theory, which is nothing more than the political side of philosophical naturalism, the family is viewed as simply a development in the evolutionary process that will pass away in time. Engels remarked that "human society arose out of a troupe of tree-climbing monkeys."[20] A book on lesbianism, reviewed in the *New York Times*, attempts to help in overcoming traditional, that is, Christian, attitudes regarding "the nuclear family, that cradle of evil."[21] Biblical norms regarding heterosexual marriage relationships have been abandoned in favor of all types of "legitimate" lifestyles: homosexuality, bestiality, and pedophilia.

14. *Government is a creation of man and is usually centralized in the State.* As with the origin of the family, civil government is also a creature of the evolutionary process. The individual is of no consequence. Those with the greatest power control. All totalitarian regimes begin with the fallacies of naturalism and degenerate into perpetrators of unspeakable atrocities. Nazi Germany was no exception: "It is thus necessary that the individual should finally come to realize that his own ego is of no importance in comparison with the existence of his nation; that the position of the individual ego is conditioned solely by the interests of the nation as a whole . . . that above all the unity of a nation's spirit and will are worth far more than the freedom of the spirit and will of an individual."[22]

15. *Human rights are subjective, transient, and created by the State.* Why should we expect the protection of fundamental rights when man is nothing more than an animal? Why should the weak be protected by the strong? With naturalism there is no reason. All talk about human rights comes from those nations that have had a Christian base. The most familiar philosophy of human rights is found in the Declaration of Independence (1776). "All men," it states, "are endowed by their Creator with certain unalienable Rights, that among these are Life, Liberty and the pursuit of Happiness."

The philosophy of rights is intimately tied to the reality of the Creator who alone grants rights. No God, no rights. The Declaration makes it clear that these inalienable rights are not granted by governments; rather, they are an *endowment*, a gift, of the Creator of the universe.[23]

On the other hand, there are the French Declaration of the Rights of Man (1789) and the more recent United Nations' Declaration of Human Rights (1948), which are indicative of *governments* as the grantors of rights. If governments can give rights they can just as easily revoke them. "The State giveth. The State taketh away. Blessed be the name of the State."

The Declaration of Independence says that "among" the many rights God has bestowed, "Life, Liberty, and the pursuit of happiness" are just three of them. The assumption is that there are more rights, but to list them would be to limit them. On the other hand, the French Declaration of the Rights of Man enumerates the rights of citizens and, thus, limits "rights" to the seventeen listed. What happens when the State decides a certain right is no longer a right?

16. *Man's environment accounts for all the "evil" in the world.* Of course, there really is no evil for the naturalist. "Good" and "evil" are nothing more than subjective categories of what people like and dislike at a given time. But the designation exists even for the naturalist, so we have to deal with it. For the naturalist, evil itself (unpleasant acts) must have a physical cause. Man's environment, the world in which he lives, is at fault. Famine, death, and man's cruelty to man can all be explained environmentally. Change a person's environment and the man will change. Give the thief enough food to eat and he will stop stealing. For the environmentalist[24] "*salvation is escape from an evil environment to a good one.* In the good environment, man will develop his physical and mental abilities in all directions."[25] In a naturalistic worldview there can be no other explanation for "evil" except the world. Sin never enters the picture.

Domino Three: Relativism

How many times have you been in a heated debate with someone over some controversial issue only to have it end with, "Well, everything is relative." End of discussion. Nothing you say can make any difference because your opponent does not believe in absolutes. (Of course, maintaining that everything is relative is an absolute statement.) Most of America's youth have been raised on the relativism doctrine.

> There is one thing a professor can be absolutely certain of: almost every student entering the university believes, or says he believes, that truth is relative. . . . The students' backgrounds are as various as America can provide. Some are religious, some

atheists; some are to the Left, some to the Right; some intend to be scientists, some humanists or professionals or businessmen; some are poor, some rich. They are unified only in their relativism and their allegiance to equality.[26]

Relativism is the offspring of naturalism. The relativistic worldview postulates that absolutes are impossible. What is wrong today can be right tomorrow. For example, prior to 1973 abortion was considered immoral and illegal, although attitudes and laws were beginning to change as far back as the mid-1960s.

Prior to 1973 the Hippocratic Oath expressed the views of most doctors. But with *Roe v. Wade* anyone who practices abortion must repudiate the statement from the Oath which prohibits a doctor from giving a pregnant woman any "deadly drug, [or] . . . a pessary [suppository] to produce an abortion." Now doctors take an oath not to "do anything illegal." How is this different from the Nazi atrocities that were perfectly "legal" according to Nazi law? The Declaration of Geneva (adopted in September 1948 by the General Assembly of the World Medical Organization), which was modeled after the Hippocratic Oath, was also used by medical school graduates. It included: "I will maintain the utmost respect for human life from the time of conception." Subsequent editions show a modified Declaration of Geneva with the removal of "from the time of conception." After the *Roe v. Wade* pro-abortion decision, abortion became moral and legal.

Fixed standards do not exist in a relativistic world. Of course, once naturalism wins the day through a relativistic philosophy, things remain fixed. The pro-abortionists would never want to admit that sometime in the future abortion could once again be made illegal. Relativism only seems to operate against a worldview that maintains absolutes. Once the old worldview is disposed of (in this case, the Christian worldview), the advocates of the new worldview do not allow others to tamper with the new order. All things are indeed relative, even the doctrine of relativism. The college campus is an institution dedicated to this absurd doctrine:

> At Harvard University in November [1986], there was yet another of those meetings where university folk discuss how to "reform" higher education. There, Cornell University President Frank H. T. Rhodes suggested it was time for universities to pay "real and sustained attention to students' intellectual and moral well-being."

THE CHRISTIAN WORLDVIEW

This elicited gasps and even catcalls from the audience of professors and students. One indignant student rose to challenge Rhodes. "Who is going to do the moral instructing?" he demanded. "Whose morality are we going to follow?" The audience applauded thunderously, believing that the student had settled the issue and shut Rhodes up simply by posing these unanswerable questions.[27]

Relativism thrives within the evolutionary worldview. Since for the naturalist nothing "governs" the universe except chance, why should we expect to find absolutes for moral decisions? And yet these same scientists will insist on absolutes when it comes to scientific experimentation and documentation of archeological specimens to support their evolutionary claims.

We see a related development in constitutional law. In an evolutionary and naturalistic universe, nothing is fixed and definite. Nothing endures over time. This includes language. We're told that there is no definite meaning in the language, for example, of the United States Constitution.[28] Thus, law becomes whatever the Supreme Court says it is.

> [This shift] began with the application of Darwinism to law—all law. Julian Huxley once noted that the evolutionary belief system encompasses the disciplines such as "law and religion . . . until we are enabled to see evolution as a universal, all pervading process. . . . Our present knowledge indeed forces us to view that the world of reality is evolution—a single process of self-transformation."[29]

What does relativism do to individuals? It paralyzes people as merely observers. The relativist can study different cultures, for example, but he cannot make a value judgment that one culture is any better than another. In the study of religion there are similar pitfalls.

CONCLUSION

Who will set the standards for determining what is real and what is illusion? Modern science has its limits. It can only discover what the scientist can see. Science may not arbitrarily dismiss what it cannot see. This is outside the bounds of science. Naturalism is a faith because it postulates in absolute terms what it cannot measure. There is a difference between what cannot be measured and what someone determines is not there to be measured.

> The naturalist's argument is no more than a sophisticated version of the anti-theistic argument of Yuri Gagarin. Emblazoned on the walls of the anti-God museum in Leningrad are Gagarin's stirring words proclaimed upon re-entry from space, roughly translated: "I have been out in space and didn't see God; therefore there is no God." Such reasoning is foolish, but it illuminates an ancient insight: A viewpoint is important because it determines what one sees, not necessarily what there is to be seen.[30]

Science can only exist when it assumes that the world is not in chaos—that there is unity, order, law—that it is intelligible, logical, and consistent. But what made it so? Did order evolve out of chaos? Did what is random become law-like and predictable?

The naturalist must assume the validity of a world created by a personal God in order for there to be any meaning in life. Of course, he will never admit this. He will assume that *meaning* itself is an evolving concept. If the naturalist were consistent with his starting point (the universe is all that is or ever will be), then he could not give meaning to anything. In fact, *meaning* would not *mean* anything. And yet, we find intelligent college professors trying to persuade tens of thousands of students every year that life as we know it is simply an accident, and yet, we *accidents* are *meaningful*. Consider the following naturalistic interpretation of man.

> The human species has inhabited this planet for only 250,000 years or so—roughly .0015 percent of the history of life, the last inch of the cosmic mile. The world fared perfectly well without us for all but the last moment of earthly time—and this makes our appearance look like an accidental afterthought than the culmination of a prefigured plan. Moreover, the pathways that have led to our evolution are quirky, improbable, unrepeatable and utterly unpredictable. Human evolution is not random; it makes sense and can be explained after the fact. But wind back life's tape to the dawn of time and let it play again—and you will never get humans a second time.
>
> We are here because one odd group of fishes had a peculiar fin anatomy that could transform into legs for terrestrial creatures; because the earth never froze entirely during an ice age; because

a small and tenuous species, arising in Africa a quarter of a million years ago, has managed, so far, to survive by hook and by crook. We may yearn for a "higher" answer—but none exists. This explanation, though superficially troubling, if not terrifying, is ultimately liberating and exhilarating. We cannot read the meaning of life passively in the facts of nature. We must construct these answers ourselves—from our own wisdom and ethical sense. There is no other way.[31]

These words of utter nonsense are the musings of Stephen Jay Gould, professor of paleontology at Harvard, the leading anti-Christian evolutionist. Is it any wonder that young people see no purpose in life? "We may yearn for a 'higher' answer—but none exists," Dr. Gould tells us. All choices are good choices, suicide and drug addiction included. We should be amazed by the logic of evolutionists when they tell us that we are nothing more than a complicated conglomeration of atoms, and at the same time we are profound enough to generate "our own wisdom and ethical sense." How does an evolved entity know what wisdom is?

4
SHOPPING FOR A GOD

> When we speak of the whole man, we know that he is more than a skeleton with meat on it. Man, created in the image of God, is a whole entity comprised of body, mind, and soul. People are spiritual beings as well as material entities. We could say that this goes without saying, but it does not. We no longer operate from the same philosophical base as earlier generations.[1]

THE physical world abhors a vacuum. Remove the water from a glass and air will rush in to take its place. You can actually hear this principle at work as you open a vacuum-packed can of coffee. The rush of air is almost immediate. Once the lid is off, the vacuum is filled with the surrounding atmosphere.

The same principle is true for man. Remove the Triune God of Scripture from his life, and you can be sure that some other god will rush in to take His place. Herbert Schlossberg, in his foundational study of contemporary idol worship, said it this way: "Western society, in turning away from the Christian faith, has turned to other things. This process is commonly called *secularization*, but that conveys only the negative aspect. The word connotes the turning away from the worship of God while ignoring the fact that something is being turned *to* in its place."[2]

Keep in mind that you are a spiritual creation. You must nourish the part of you that the Bible describes as your "spirit." Just as there are all types of food for the body, there is food for the soul or spirit, "spiritual food" (1 Corinthians 10:3). But not just any food will meet the nutritional demands required by your spirit. Just as there is "junk food" that can rob your body of essential nutrients and can turn a healthy body into an anemic one, there are all types of spiritual junk foods that can wreck your spiritual health. If you don't eat the right spiritual food, you will starve to death or you will seek any nourishment that promises to satisfy your hunger.

The American public has sensed that something has been missing from discussions when man and his needs are discussed. In a recent survey of eighty thousand of its readers, *Better Homes and Gardens* learned some startling things about the belief patterns of its subscribers. But what was most notable was the recognition that the media, our nation's largest source of speedy and seemingly accurate information, are ignoring man's spiritual needs. This comment is representative:

> I am answering your questionnaire because I believe you have hit upon a part of our nature that too often is neglected in secular magazines. The physical and mental faculties are discussed in depth, but, in essence, they depend on our spiritual well-being. I think religion plays a far more important role in many families than most of the media realize.[3]

The spiritual spectrum of the survey varies widely: from "New Age" Spiritualists to Christian "Fundamentalists." Most believe in eternal life (eighty-nine percent), heaven (eighty-seven percent), miracles (eighty-six percent), and hell (seventy-six percent). But some believe in non-Christian doctrines like a spiritual/astral realm (thirty percent), channeling messages/lessons from spirits (thirteen percent), and reincarnation (eleven percent).[4] The survey showed that people crave spiritual things. For some, almost any type of spirituality will do. As one respondent wrote, "Faith is what you believe in."[5] But what is that "what"?

In this chapter we will look at what conditions make it easy for people to be seduced by spiritual counterfeits and what you can do to avoid being seduced by false prophets, promises, and messiahs.

THE SMORGASBORD MENTALITY

People are so confused about what is true that they tend to believe *anything* and *everything*. Students today are given "options," with no consideration that one of the many options under study could be correct. In fact, it seems to be an unwritten law among teachers not to say "this is right" or "this is wrong." It's fashionable to have an open mind. Like an open sewer, you never know what will drain there. Our society has moved from absolutism to an undiscerning openness. "Openness—and the relativism that makes it the only plausible stance in the face of various claims to truth and various ways of life and kinds of human beings—is the great insight of our times. The true believer is the real danger."[6]

The true believer is the outcast. A belief in norms, absolutes, and certainty is undemocratic. The student who enters college with an uncritical open mind will find himself swept away by every wind of doctrine, every appealing opinion, and every spiritual counterfeit to fill the spiritual vacuum. The doctrine of pluralism is the key that will be used to open your vacuum-packed mind.

> Pluralism refers to a diversity of religions, worldviews, and ideologies existing at one time in the same society. We are socially heterogeneous. One religion or philosophy doesn't command and control the culture. Instead, many viewpoints exist. We have Buddhists and Baptists, Christian Reformed and Christian Scientist—all on the same block, or at least in the same city. This can have a leveling effect on religious faith.[7]

Our nation is steeped in pluralism, tolerance, diversity, freedom, and the "democratic spirit."[8] All lifestyles are permitted. Homosexuality is tolerated because we live in a "diverse society." Abortion is legal because "you cannot impose your morality on someone else who has a different set of moral standards." The only view that is not tolerated is the view that does not tolerate all views. Christianity came on the scene with Jesus saying, "I am *the* way and *the* truth and *the* life; *no one comes to the Father but by Me*" (John 14:6). How intolerant of Him to exclude Mayan spirits, the Buddha, Mohammed, and just plain decent folk!

> Modern pluralism presents one prevailing opinion about Jesus Christ. Like all great religious leaders, he is special but not unique; and he is certainly not exclusive. That would be closed- and narrow-minded. He is classed with the multitude of masters, grouped with the gurus, but not exalted as supreme. He is tucked into a comfortable corner of the religious pantheon so as to disturb no one.

> The assumption is that Jesus just couldn't have claimed to be the only way; that's undemocratic! So instead of facing Christ's challenge as it stands, the whole idea is dismissed as anti-pluralistic, and closed-minded.[9]

There can be no true religion over against all false religions. Christianity is *a* religion but not *the* religion. The Bible can *sometimes* be taught as fictional literature like Shakespeare, but it cannot be taught as the Word of God. This would offend Moslems, Buddhists, Mormons,[10] and most certainly atheists. Unsuspecting students are then open to any and all philosophical gurus who are ready, willing, and seemingly able to lead the way to a new vision of reality. New worldviews are a dime a dozen. Those best able to express their views get the greatest following.

FROM RATIONALISM TO IRRATIONALITY

Christianity is rational.* Surprised? Well, you shouldn't be. The Christian faith offers the most rational explanation of why man and the universe operate the way they do.

> **Rational*: What pertains to and satisfies man's intellect. This should be distinguished from "rationalism" (the view that man's autonomous reason is his final authority).

As Christians we do not take a leap into the void of irrationality when we decide to believe in God and the authority of His Word although there are people who believe that religion, any religion, is simply one way to make people feel good and to give them a sense of security and meaning. The skeptic might say something like this: "Some people turn to drugs and alcohol, others 'get religion.'" The sad thing is, many people do turn to religion, all types of religions, to make them feel good. For the religious experimenters, there is no real understanding of Biblical Christianity. One religion is as good as any other. Jonestown taught us otherwise.

The Lesson of Jonestown

Why would nine hundred men, women, and children voluntarily take a lethal dose of cyanide-laced Kool-Aid? In November 1978 the nation viewed the horror of nine hundred bloated bodies lying peacefully in the remote jungle of Guyana, South America. There was no sign of a struggle. For these people and the families they left behind, it does matter "what" one believes. But what led these people to so unite with a religious leader like Jim Jones that they were willing to go with him to their deaths? A letter left behind by one of the suicide victims tells it all.

> For my part—I am more than tired of this wretched, merciless planet and the hell it holds for so many masses of beautiful people—thank you [Jim Jones] for the only life I've known.[11]

These desperate people saw something in Jim Jones that for a time filled a spiritual void. When it seemed the only hope they had ever had was going to be ripped from their very beings, they ended it all. Death was better than facing life with a spiritual void that could not be filled. For them, religion was nothing more than a personal harbor from a mounting storm.

Christianity is not a crutch or simply a haven for the restless. The Christian faith brings rebellious and hell-bound sinners into a right relationship with the Creator of the universe. Christianity works in the real world just because it is true. It explains why things are the way they are and what can be done to change man and creation for the better. Therefore, the Christian faith can be put to the test in the real world. Of course, this should be distinguished from unprincipled "pragmatism," where something is tried with little or no regard to absolutes. There is no guarantee that anything will work in the worldview of pragmatism.

The presuppositions that we hold regarding God, the Bible, and our ultimate destiny will work in the real world. Deep in his heart, Jim Jones knew that his religion could not weather the storms of life. His unprincipled pragmatic program, "Jonestown," lost. His only way out was in death.

How does the rationalist know for certain that his worldview is the right one? What will happen to the rationalist after death? Is the grave the end? Or is there a hell? He can never know outside of Christ and His Word. A worldview whose foundation is pure unaided rationality can never offer certainty. C. S. Lewis, in an address to the Oxford Socratic Club (1944), shows that the naturalistic worldview invariably reduces itself to skepticism:

> If . . . I swallow the scientific cosmology as a whole, then not only can I not fit in Christianity, but I cannot even fit in science. If minds are wholly dependent on brains and brains on bio-chemistry, and bio-chemistry (in the long run) on the meaningless flux of the atoms, I cannot understand how the thought of those minds should have any more significance than the sound of the wind in the trees.[12]

There is no certainty for the finite creature who attempts to interpret the world from his limited perspective. And there were no answers in the irrational world of Jim Jones. The irrational act of suicide proved little and offered nothing for those who so much wanted to hope and believe that everything would be all right.

DEFINING OUR TERMS

We should, at this point, define and contrast the terms *rationality*, *rationalism*, and *irrationality*. There are many irrational people who believe they are quite rational within the context of their worldview. Jim Jones was "rationally" carrying out the implications of his worldview. Suicide was the most "rational" thing to do, seeing that his world was about to be destroyed. In this use of rational, it is synonymous with "consistency." Jones followed the implications of his worldview to its "consistent" end. Those who reject the Christian faith also believe that they are doing so on purely "rational" grounds. But within the context of the Christian worldview, their actions are completely irrational as we will demonstrate. The following definitions are formulated within the bounds of the Christian worldview.

Rationality: Thinking God's Thoughts After Him

Rationality, the ability to think and reason, is a gift from God. The rational person makes accurate assessments of his world based on the facts at hand. A burner on a stove cannot be hot and cold at the same time. It can be warm, but this is neither hot nor cold. A rational person would not test his hypothesis every time the burner was turned on. If it did not turn red, he would assume that it was not turned up high enough to glow or that there might be a malfunction. He would test his reasoning by placing his hand over the burner at a safe distance. This is the process of rationality in action. It is not guesswork.

To state this more formally, the rational man applies the law of non-contradiction on a consistent basis; that is, "Nothing can be both A and not-A *at the same time and in the same respect*."[13] Refusal to live in terms of this principle will lead to skepticism. God cannot lie, so logical consistency is necessary for God's reasoning creature, man.

Let's go back to our burner. It can be hot, warm, or cold. But it cannot be hot, warm, and cold *at the same time*. To think that it can be all three at the same time can lead to a badly burned hand if a bright red burner is not seen as an indicator of high temperature.

SHOPPING FOR A GOD

Now, there may be things that cannot be *explained* rationally; that is, man's intellect cannot understand or explain all that is true (known by God). But this does not necessarily mean that these unexplainables are not true. There are scientists who work with theories without having all the facts to support the theory conclusively. Scientists are being rational even though they can't determine why something works the way it does. They would be abandoning rationality, however, if a theory did not work but they continued to use it as if it did. All of us work in terms of some ignorance. We don't know everything. "Ideas are everywhere, but knowledge is rare. Even a so-called 'knowledgeable' person usually has solid knowledge only within some special area, representing a tiny fraction of the whole spectrum of human concerns. Humorist Will Rogers said, 'Everybody is ignorant, only on different subjects.'"[14]

A rational person is someone who works on the basis of available evidence. If I know that I have $200.00 in my checking account, and yet operate in terms of having $300.00 in my account, I am being irrational (and sinful). Of course, I could be operating in terms of inaccurate evidence. I could be acting rational, that is, in terms of the available evidence I have, but I could be wrong. Therefore,

> [A] rational belief is not necessarily a true one. When a jury finds someone guilty in light of the evidence, it is still possible that the person is innocent, even if the more reasonable view (on the basis of the evidence) is that he is guilty. . . . Truth does not change. Something either is or is not true. A rational belief can be changed when new evidence comes in.[15]

Rationality is the characteristic of man by which he uses his intellect to explain, predict, or control the world around and within him. A cook must presuppose that a bright red burner means "very hot," and he must believe that it will be so tomorrow. He places his confidence, faith if you will, in such predictability. Try studying for a test without a belief in a predictable (cause-effect) universe. A poor performance on a test will *cause* you to get a poor grade. You can *predict* that if you don't know the answers to the test, you will not do well. These presuppositions, controlling the use of reason as a tool, get you through life. Reason, then, is a God-given tool to discover how the world works. It is not the unaided criterion for truth itself; that is, reason serves the court, but it is not the final judge.

Rationalism: Thinking Man's Thoughts After Him

Rationalism takes an extreme position regarding man's ability to think and reason logically. For the rationalist, *autonomous* reason is considered the only criterion for real knowledge and understanding. Reason supposedly explains everything that can be explained. The rationalist does not consider revelation as a source or a vehicle of knowledge. Revelation is outside the bounds of "rational" discussion since it is not based on the authority of man's mind. Even if revelation existed, we could not understand or apply any of its propositions.

Anti-Christian worldviews have boasted in the presupposition that the world can be explained in terms of autonomous reason alone. In the minds of the rationalists, there is always a "rational" explanation for all that happens; that is, one acceptable to man's mind. There is no need to postulate, for example, that God created the universe and man. The origin of man can be explained adequately in terms of evolution. But can it? Can evolution explain love, compassion, grief, and hope? Is it any wonder that drug and shock therapy (and at one time lobotomies) have been used to treat "mental illness"? You see, there must be some "organic" reason for a person's problems. In a purely materialistic, naturalistic, and rationalistic worldview these emotions and mental disturbances cannot exist.

But experience teaches every man, woman, and child that these feelings do exist. We base our lives on the belief that *love* is real and unique to humans. Our halls of justice cry out to have *compassion* on the poor. As a nation we *grieve* as we visit the Vietnam Memorial in Washington, D.C. where the names of tens of thousands of dead soldiers are chiseled in granite for all the world to see. We *hope* that in the future the names of our children will not be immortalized in a similar way.

Basically, rationalism assumes that man is the final court of appeal when declaring what is true or false. If it cannot be explained by man and his reasoning abilities, then it cannot be true or it does not exist. For the rationalist, reason is the criterion for truth. But there are some things that the instruments of science just cannot measure.

THE MANY FACES OF IRRATIONALISM

There must be a way to account for all the "unexplainables," those things that just don't fit within the context of a materialistic, naturalistic, and rationalistic worldviews. The rationalist, if he is consistent with his reason-alone premise, has no ultimate answers to life's basic questions:

SHOPPING FOR A GOD

How did the world get here?
Who am I?
Is there any meaning to life?
What will happen to me when I die?
Are there any moral absolutes?
Is there any meaning to history?

How can the rationalist answer these questions with any certainty? Humanistic rationalism has forsaken the Christian worldview that has answers to all these questions. The rationalist can guess at an answer, but he can never know for sure. And if he is consistent with his rationalism, he really has no answers. In fact, it doesn't really matter if he asks the questions at all.

But few people are satisfied with rationalistic and naturalistic answers. There is more to man than the explanation that he is a highly evolved amalgamation of atoms. A better explanation must be sought from something greater than man. If the God of the Bible is not chosen, then rationalistic man drifts into the realm of the irrational. The rationalist throws reason to the wind for just enough time to salvage his rationalistic worldview. Two polar opposites—rationalism and irrationalism—join forces to solve the mysteries of the universe. They are surely an unlikely pair. The rationalist believes that all things can be explained and defined in terms of reason alone. But reason cannot explain all things. Leaps of irrationality become necessary to keep rationalism from disintegrating.

There is a "secret treaty" between rationalism and irrationalism in which the reason-alone worldview accepts irrational explanations of how the world might work to explain what scientism and naturalism cannot.[16]

Looking for ET

Consider this bit of irrationality from the minds of the rationalists. For over a hundred years—at least since the publication of Darwin's *Origin of Species* in 1859—scientists and skeptics in general have worked to shove God out of the universe. But in the past few decades, the theistic skeptics have once again turned their eyes and ears toward the heavens—not to seek for God, but to hope for a message from outer space, from a higher life form, for some "explanation" for the way the universe works. They are hoping there is something out there to give our existence meaning. Some have gone so far as to assert that our earth was visited by extraterrestrials thousands of years ago. In these visitations, primitive earthlings were given highly advanced medical, technical, and architectural skills, and, thus, mankind made tremendous leaps in evolutionary development. Eric Von Daniken argues this thesis in several books that have sold millions of copies: *In Search of Ancient Gods*, *Chariots of the Gods?*, *The Gold of the Gods*, and *Gods from Outer Space*.

Some scientists are going to great lengths to search for more highly evolved extraterrestrial life forms. The *Pioneer* and *Voyager* space probes were designed to search for life after the *Viking* mission to Mars turned up a dead planet. If *Viking* had found life on Mars it would have given the naturalists and rationalists the evidence they needed to push the idea of God further out of the universe and support for their unfounded faith in evolution. "It would have brought the question of the origin of life fully into the domain of science. . . . Believers in evolution in the fall of 1976 could only wish for one message from *Viking*—the demonstration of life on Mars."[17] They didn't get it.

The *Pioneer 10* and *11* and *Voyager 1* and *2* flights did not test the possibility of life on other planets. Instead, each of the crafts "carr[ied] long-playing records that contain[ed] electronically encoded pictures of Earth, as well as spoken greetings, sound effects, and a selection of music from around the world."[18] So much is done to prove that extraterrestrial intelligence (ETI) exists, while nothing is done with the insurmountable evidence of God's existence. Carl Sagan, for example, has dismissed God in spite of his own admission that "the size and age of the Cosmos are beyond ordinary human understanding."[19] How can insignificant man on an insignificant planet in an insignificant galaxy make a dogmatic statement about the non-existence of God? His dogmatism in the light of his own insignificance still leads him to proclaim the following in the opening line to his multimillion-selling *Cosmos*: "The Cosmos is all that is or ever was or ever will be."[20] Even so, he speculates wildly about the possibility, not of God, but of extraterrestrial intelligence.

> In the Milky Way Galaxy there must be many planets millions of years older than Earth, and some that are billions of years older. Should we not have been visited? In all the billions of years since the origin of our planet, has there not been even once a strange craft from a distant civilization surveying our world from above, and slowly settling down to the surface to be observed by iridescent dragonflies, incurious reptiles, screeching primates or wondering humans?[21]

SHOPPING FOR A GOD

In spite of Sagan's admission that there are "no compelling cases of extraterrestrial visitation,"[22] he still probes the cosmos for evidence. Rational thought is discarded for a cosmic seance. He ends *Cosmos* with this: "*We* speak for earth. Our obligation to survive is owed not just to ourselves but also to that Cosmos, ancient and vast, from which we spring."[23] But he doesn't dare ask the next most rational question: From whence sprang the cosmos? Sagan is satisfied with the fact that it just is.

Earlier in *Cosmos*, Sagan attempts to dismiss the need to postulate God. With a bit of semantic sleight of hand he tries to convince his readers that the idea of God creating the universe is no more significant than a belief in Santa Claus or the Tooth Fairy. It's all right to discuss the question, but there really is no need for His existence. Sagan approvingly quotes a ninth-century Indian philosopher: "Some foolish men declare that a Creator made the world. The doctrine that the world was created is ill-advised, and should be rejected. If God created the world, where was He before creation? . . . How could God have made the world without any raw material? If you say He made this first, and then the world, you are faced with an endless regression. . . . Know that the world is uncreated, as time itself, without beginning and end."[24]

The belief that God created the world out of nothing and the belief that the world is uncreated are faith propositions. Neither can be proved scientifically because no one was there when it happened, except God, of course. In Sagan's worldview—God's testimony does not count. Rather, the views of a ninth-century Indian philosopher and the conclusions of twentieth-century minds that cannot come up with a cure for the common cold are considered definitive in their assertions. Sagan is certain that "ten or twenty billion years ago, something happened." But he doesn't know "why it happened."[25]

So what does Sagan do to resolve the "greatest mystery we know"?[26] He junks scientific rationalism and jumps into the universe of irrationalism.

> In many cultures it is customary to answer that God created the universe out of nothing. But this is mere temporizing. If we wish courageously to pursue the question, we must of course ask next where God comes from. And if we decide this to be unanswerable, why not save a step and decide that the origin of the universe is an unanswerable question. Or, if we say that God always existed, why not save a step and conclude that the universe has always existed?[27]

Is this science? Why not "save a step" in a scientific experiment? No scientist would dare suggest such a thing. Why not have your surgeon "save a step" in the operating room, or your mechanic "save a step" on your brake job. No one would ever suggest saving a step in these little things—little in terms of the vastness of the cosmos and the question of its origin—but not little in terms of losing your life. Without God nothing in science counts as an explanation or proof. Stop with the universe and you don't have *it* understood either.

The origin of the universe is one of the most important questions one can ask, especially if the answer is found in a personal God who holds man accountable for his sin. But Carl Sagan is willing to adopt irrationalism at this most crucial point. He is willing to dismiss Pascal's "Wager":

> If God exists and punishes unbelief, you will be punished in the hereafter if you do not believe.
>
> If God does not exist, there is no reward for belief but neither is there a penalty.

Of course, Pascal's "Wager" is not a very satisfying argument for belief in God. But Sagan has bet his soul on the unproven assumption that there is no need to postulate God. Without belief in God, one cannot justify acting or thinking in terms of this as a "Cosmos" (orderly and predictable), thus one cannot justify science. God is "needed" for science's methodology to be cogent. Sagan is willing to adopt irrationalism rather than to believe the most rational proposition of them all: "In the beginning God created the heavens and the earth" (Genesis 1:1). With Sagan's worldview, we are left with non-life giving birth to life, an impersonal universe giving rise to personality, chaos spawning order, and randomness generating predictability.

Where does the leap into irrationality take us? The answer is clear. With God shoved out of the universe man becomes the new god. Man now gives meaning to the evolutionary designs of the cosmos.

> Through billions of years of blind mutation, pressing against the shifting walls of their environment, microbes finally emerged as man. We are no longer blind; at least we are beginning to be conscious of what has happened and of what may happen. From now on, evolution is what we make it.[28]

At one time it was reasonable to believe without contradicting true science that an omnipotent and personal God created the universe. Now it's reasonable to believe that finite and fallible man, a mere compound of atoms, will one day control the direction of the universe. Irrationality has replaced rationality with a vengeance.

Save the Whales But Not the Babies

Irrationality is not unique to science. Irrational leaps work themselves out in the day-to-day thinking of ethicists and special interest groups as well. The radical environmental group "Greenpeace," for example, will work for legislation to save the whales and baby seals, but will not take a stand on abortion. The eggs of the nearly extinct American bald eagle have more legal protection than an unborn baby. When man wants to play god, all ethical norms are thrown out the window, except those that support, say, a political agenda or a deviant lifestyle. But it's irrational to believe that the eggs of a bald eagle are worthy of protection under the law, but the fertilized egg of a woman is not. The worldview of rationalism needs the leaps of irrationality to "explain" the unexplainable. Thus, the rationalistic worldview is willing to kill some human beings

> for their own good or that of others and is even able to place some of them below the status of animals. While stressing the special worth of human beings, it says they must not be kept alive if that would cost too much. Deeming people worthy of support and help when they are needy, humanism reduces their actions to automatic responses to the environment, like those of animals and machines.[29]

If AIDS were Only a Brand of Cigarette

Such irrationality is always current. Take the AIDS epidemic. Compare the advertisements to get the word out that people should stop smoking cigarettes, dipping snuff, chewing tobacco, and taking drugs because of their *potentially* lethal effects and that of the *always* lethal AIDS virus. What are young people told to do as they face the lure of alcohol, tobacco products, and drugs?: "Just say No!" But this won't do with the lethal AIDS virus. Why? Because AIDS is a disease most often transmitted by sodomy, and sodomy is practiced by men who reject God, especially a God who mandates laws against sodomy. So then it is best to act irrationally than to admit that AIDS kills.

CONCLUSION

Some men will go to great lengths to escape their Creator. But there's no place to hide. No one gets out of this world alive. Death is the great equalizer. Even in life there is no escape from God's world. The Psalmist writes:

> Where can I go from Thy Spirit? Or where can I flee from Thy presence? If I ascend to heaven, Thou art there; if I make my bed in Sheol, behold, Thou art there. If I take the wings of the dawn, if I dwell in the remotest part of the sea, even there Thy hand will lead me, and Thy right hand will lay hold of me, and the light around me will be night (Psalm 139:7-10).

Rebels against God hope to create a world in which God is not needed. Carl Sagan has concluded: "As we learn more and more about the universe, there seems less and less for God to do."[30] Can this be? Or is it true that without God, man is nothing?

Not only is man nothing without God, there is no future without God. Where can man without God set his hopes? What assurances does he have that there will be a tomorrow? A universe devoid of a personal creator is no universe. A universe requires a unifying principle to hold it together. Naturalism has nothing to offer but chaos. This is why the naturalistic worldview called humanism is in disrepair. Even humanistic critics see it. They still hope for a better tomorrow, but if the past is any indicator of the things to come, then we are all destined to a postmortem world. The litany of pessimism is displayed for us in the works of historians and social critics. News broadcasts bring the results of a consistent naturalistic worldview into our living rooms each evening.

Even humanists see pessimism for Western culture as it increasingly embraces secular humanism.

- The end of the Roman Empire was a minor event compared with what we behold. We are looking at the liquidation of what is known as the "modern world."
- Civilization is collapsing before our eyes.
- I have to report the affairs of a world which has lost its faith, which is like a fish out of water or a drowning man, desperately thrashing around for lack of oxygen. Since the time of Christ there has been no period in which there has been the same feeling of . . . spiritual impoverishment.

- Civilization is collapsing before our eyes.
- The vision of Utopia was suddenly replaced by the specter of Doomsday.[31]

Remember, this is humanists' evaluation of their unfulfilled prophecies of optimism. It is their own commentary on the belief in the inevitability of progress generated by the wit and wisdom of man. Humanistic thought, in its denial of God and God's coherent world, is like a clay pot which will be dashed to pieces (Psalm 2:9). In essence, humanism is self-destructive.

5
LEAPING INTO THE VOID

> Because of the prestige of science as a source of power, and because of the general neglect of philosophy, the popular [world-and-life view] of our times contains a large element of what may be called "nothing-but" thinking. Human beings, it is more or less tacitly assumed, are nothing but bodies, animals, even machines. . . . Values are nothing but illusions that somehow got themselves mixed up with our experience of the world.[1]

OUR culture grew up with the belief that reason, science, and technology would solve all of man's problems. When time revealed however, that these God-given tools, which had themselves been turned into gods, would not perform as gods, the disenchanted turned on them in an irrational fit of rage. The disenchanted became more and more consistent with the worldview handed down to them by the rationalists: There is no real meaning to life, the brain cannot be trusted, there is no help in science and technology, because man is "nothing but" an animal, and all values are mere illusions.

The beginning of the twentieth century brought with it the hope for unchallenged optimism. H. G. Wells, the author of the popular science fiction thrillers *The Time Machine* and *War of the Worlds*, described in his *Outline of History* (1920) a period of "evolutionary idealism, faith in progress, and complete optimism."[2] But it wasn't long before this optimism turned to despair. Shortly before his death, Wells "wrote an aptly-titled book, *The Mind at the End of Its Tether* (1945) in which he concluded that 'there is no way out, or around, or through the impasse. It is the end.'"[3]

World War I was to be the war to end all wars. The dream was never realized. The machinery of war was heard again less than twenty years later. The sons of World War I veterans fought again in desperation to realize the dream that this would be the war to end all wars. But World War II brought with it a weapon that could end all life. Technology, it seemed, was not enough. Science was not the savior it was thought to be. Something was wrong with *man*. This "defect" could not be corrected by an appeal to reason or continued advances in science and technology. What some men designed for good, other men intended for evil.

> Nuclear energy can be used to light cities or reduce them to ashes. Chemistry can improve nutrition or make nerve gas. Biology can make vaccinations or germ weapons. Science furnishes neither truth nor moral values.[4]

Man had put his trust in technology and the Darwinian worldview. But man was becoming less than man through the entire process. The atrocities of Stalin and Hitler revealed in stark detail how despotic and cruel the impersonal worldview of naturalism could be. It is no accident that Communism and Nazism claim Darwin as their patron saint. Darwin's naturalistic and mechanistic approach to origins found an immediate response in Karl Marx (1818-1883) and his successors, Lenin and Stalin. Darwin's *Origin of Species* "is the book," Marx wrote to his disciple Engels in 1866, "which contains the basis in natural history for our view."[5] There are no absolutes, man is nothing, and the State is everything. For Communism, the advancement of the State is the march of god through the world. Communism insures this through raw power, the Gulag, and the "necessary" extinction of millions to bring the "ideals" of Communism to the masses. It is significant to note that "after 1949 when the communists took control of China, the first new text introduced to all the schools was neither Marxist or Leninist, but Darwinian."[6] With Darwin, all things are permissible.

In a *Time* magazine cover of April 8, 1966, this question was asked: "Is God Dead?" In the minds of the naturalists, He had been dead a long time. It seemed that all the failed ideologies of naturalism, rationalism, and materialism had come home to roost. Those who denied the supernatural were ecstatic. But it took only three-and-a-half years for *Time* to ask another question: "Is God coming back to life?" (December 26,

LEAPING INTO THE VOID

1969). Religious man could not live for long in the shadow of the God-is-Dead "theology." He had to escape the world of cold rationalism. One way was to leap into the void of irrationalism. Man needed a god. Some god. Any god.

> Theodore Roszak has described the irrationalism of the youth counter culture of the 1960s in *The Making of a Counter Culture*. The "flower generation" staged a neo-romantic revolt against science, technology, and reason in favor of feeling, sexuality, drugs, rock music, fantasy, and Eastern Mysticism. The new heaven of peace, love, and freedom failed to materialize as expected, but the arational experientalism of these years lingers on in a younger generation of Americans.[7]

After so many years of having a naturalistic worldview dominate our culture, the results have been, ironically, just the opposite of what the rationalists expected. The rebellion of the youth on the college campus in the past few decades was a revolt against the impersonal treatment of man. The counter culture's depiction of reality as "plastic" was an accurate one. A rationalistic universe ruled solely by impersonal and non-purposed physical forces does not generate feeling, compassion, or moral restraint. Without God, everything human succumbs to the random control of impersonal mechanisms.

But, the rejection of one god brings with it the choking embrace of another. What did the disenchanted adopt after their rationalistic worldview failed to meet their God-implanted needs? The craving was not fulfilled by the insistence that the universe is all there is or ever will be. Some substitute had to be found. Irrationalism seemed to open the door to a vast new world that unveiled countless possibilities and innumerable pitfalls. It was a leap into the void.

THE ANTI-PHILOSOPHIES

Rationalism failed to give meaning to man in naturalism. (There is no mind or thought. Man is machine-like.) Rationalism is a leap of faith. How can we trust a brain that evolved by chance? Subjectivism failed to give meaning to man in existentialism. (With subjectivism there are no absolutes. Man can only authenticate *himself*.) Subjectivism is also a leap of faith. Who's to say that "authentication" is authentic? What is man to do?

Rationality and logic must be done away with. They are of no use to man now. The nonrational and nonlogical become the goal of the leap of faith. In the world of rationalism, "on the basis of all reason, man as man is dead. You have simply mathematics, particulars, mechanics. Man has no meaning, no purpose, no significance. There is only pessimism concerning man as man. But up above, on the basis of a nonrational, nonreasonable leap, there is nonreasonable faith which gives optimism."[8]

Eastern Mysticism

Man must take a leap of "nonreasonable faith" in the monistic worldview of eastern mysticism. What makes eastern mysticism the choice of a new generation of religious seekers, and how does it fulfill man's spiritual hunger?

1. *Eastern mysticism is nonrational and borders on the irrational.* In Zen Buddhism, for example, one's intuition is pitted against one's reason. The Hindus consider the mind to have all the stability and perception of a "drunken monkey" while the Hare Krishnas refer to the mind as a "garbage pail." All this might seem contradictory to the Western mind, and it is. But remember that the West has given up on rational explanations for the way the world works. Maybe East is best. If man is nothing more than a machine, why should we hold rationality in such high regard anyway? Western rationalism has failed.

> Perhaps another reason behind the popular abandonment of rationalism in the West is its inability to provide spiritual satisfaction. As Zen master D. T. Suzuki explains, "Zen has come to the definite conclusion that the ordinary logical process of reasoning is powerless to give final satisfaction to our deepest spiritual needs."[9]

We are often confused by the incessant chanting and the intellectual void associated with meditation on a mandala or some other fixed image. But these are simply the ways of the East. Much of Eastern thought is without intellectual content and meaning. The goal is to transcend the world of things and to reach a spiritual world beyond. The point is not to understand but only to do. This is the appeal of the East. The Western reliance on rationalism has failed. In the West, the law of non-contradiction reigned (A is not non-A). The East knows nothing of such distinctions. In Western rationalist terms, "to know reality is to distinguish one thing from another, label it, catalog it, recognize its subtle relation to other objects in the cosmos. In the East to 'know' reality is to pass beyond distinction, to 'realize' the oneness of all being one with the all."[10]

2. *Eastern mysticism is monistic.* The Christian believes in a *personal* God who is separate from His creation. We have called this the Creator/creature distinction. God did not create the world out of Himself, using the "stuff" of His own being to bring the universe and man into existence.[11] "By faith we understand that the worlds were prepared by the *word of God*, so that what is seen *was not made out of the things which are visible*" (Hebrews 11:3; cf. Genesis 1:1-2).

Eastern thought makes no distinction between man and cosmos. The name for this is *monism*. Monism "is the belief that all that is, is one. All is interrelated, interdependent and interpenetrating. Ultimately there is no difference between God, a person, a carrot or a rock."[12] Consider the ethical implications of such a view. The way you treat a person and the way you treat an animal are to be no different. This is why many advocates of monism are vegetarian. An animal is sacred; therefore, it cannot be killed for food. All is one. God and evil transcend the world of forms and plurality. God does not overcome evil. There is no value judgment in "good" and "evil." Ultimate reality is beyond good and evil. These rational and Christian concepts must be jettisoned in favor of an undifferentiated oneness.

The entertainment business has been quick to pick up on monism. In the *Star Wars* series, monism is quite evident in "the Force," a neutral entity that neither condones the good nor suppresses the evil. The music industry was invaded in the early sixties by the Beatles who held a monistic worldview.

> In 1967, the Beatles made their now-famous link-up with a then-unknown guru, Maharishi Yogi and his occult-sounding product, Transcendental Meditation. In that same year Paul McCartney and John Lennon wrote "I am the Walrus" which opened with the pantheistic declaration: "I am he as you are he as you are me and we are all together." "Instant Karma" followed in 1970 and the next year saw the release of George Harrison's "My Sweet Lord" with its alternating chorus of "Hallelujah" and "Hare Krishna."[13]

Charles Manson adopted the monistic worldview of the Beatles, and at the LaBianca murder scene in 1969, he scrawled in blood on the refrigerator door the misspelled "He[a]lter Skelter," a song title from the Beatles' *White Album*. The ambiguity of right and wrong became a reality for Manson. In Manson's words, "If God is One, what is bad?"

3. *All is god.* It follows from monism that if there is god, then all is god. Pantheism (*pan* means all; *theos* means god) is the theology of the East. There is no personal God who stands above creation. In fact, there is no creation as such. To speak of a creation would mean to postulate a Creator, someone distinct from the cosmos. Thus, the pantheist agrees with the naturalist that there is just one level of reality, although the naturalist would not consider it to be "spiritual" or "divine." In pantheism, there is no God who is "out there." God and the material world are one and the same. The word god should be used to refer to the sum total of reality rather than to some being distinct from the rest of reality.

In Christianity, God is distinct from creation. God is certainly present *with* His creation, but He is in no way a *part of* creation. To destroy the created order would in no way affect God. "The Creator God is not an impersonal force, energy or consciousness, but a living, personal Being of infinite intelligence, power and purity. God is not an amoral entity, but a moral agent who says 'Thou shalt not' and calls people to repentance and faith."[14]

4. *We are god.* The consistency of monism brings us to one of its most bizarre features. If all is god, then man is god in some form. "Swami Muktananda—a great influence on Werner Erhard, founder of est and Forum—pulls no pantheistic punches when he says: 'Kneel to your own self. Honor and worship your own being. God dwells within you as You!' "[15]

Eastern mysticism teaches some form of "chain of being" or "continuity of being,"[16] the idea that man and God are one essence, and that in time, through an evolutionary process or a series of reincarnations, man becomes divine. Ray Sutton writes:

> Life according to this system is a *continuum*. At the top is the purest form of deity. At the very bottom is the least pure. They only differ in *degree*, not in kind. God is a *part of* creation. Man, who is somewhere in the middle of the continuum, is god in another "form." In other words, god is just a "super" man, and man is not a god . . . yet![17]

Of course, Christianity teaches that there is only one God: "And you are My witnesses. Is there any God besides Me, or is there any other Rock? I know of none" (Isaiah 44:8). Man's first sin was the attempt to "be like God," determining good and evil for himself (Genesis 3:5).

5. *There is no death.* Eastern mysticism makes its "leap of being" from mere man to god through raising the state of consciousness, evolu-

tionary development, reincarnation, or some combination of the three. Death is simply the final stage of growth; it is an illusion. Human beings, because they are of a "divine essence," are immortal. Ultimately, death does not exist. For death to exist would mean the extinction of part of the One.

Reincarnation is a fundamental pillar of New Age thinking. It "solves" the puzzle of death. Reincarnation has been popularized over the years through the writings of Edgar Cayce[18] and most recently, Shirley MacLaine. The Eastern variety of reincarnation would have never been accepted in the Christian West if it had not been stripped of the hideous concept of the "transmigration of the soul."

Reincarnation, as it is usually understood in Hinduism, states that all life is essentially one (monism): plant, animal, and human life are so interrelated that souls are capable of "transmigrating" from one form of life to another. A person could have been an animal, plant, or mineral in some previous existence. However, this version is unpalatable to American tastes, so in the newer version the movement of human souls is limited to human bodies.[19]

Modern proponents of reincarnation have cleaned up the Eastern variety. You don't hear Shirley MacLaine telling people that she was a rock or a slug in a former life. The typical reincarnationist usually believes that he was once some exotic personality. This is not true reincarnationism. This is "I've always been a star" reincarnationism.

6. *Monism has spawned the New Age movement.* John Naisbitt of *Megatrends*[20] fame sees a new age dawning at the corporation level. Old industrial structures must be dismantled to compete in the information society of the future. "Look at how far we have already come. The industrial society transformed workers into consumers; the information society is transforming employees into capitalists. But remember this: Both capitalism and socialism were industrial structures. And the companies re-inventing themselves are already evolving toward that new reality."[21] But there's more!

Mark Satin has described a *New Age Politics*[22] that will "heal self and society."

Fritjof Capra, author of *The Turning Point*,[23] sees changes in science that will affect society and culture.

Marilyn Ferguson, whose *The Aquarian Conspiracy*[24] is considered by many to be the manifesto of the New Age movement, describes "a new mind—a turnabout in consciousness, a network powerful enough to bring about radical change in our culture."

Much of this literature is rooted in Eastern and occult philosophy, which emphasize oneness (monism): the unity and interdependence of all things. There is a clever mix between Eastern religious philosophy and Western religious forms. The sixties counter culture brought the esoteric music and religious ideology of the East into the West. The Beatles made Eastern music popular on their *Rubber Soul* album when George Harrison introduced the Indian sitar music of Ravi Shankar.[25] Transcendental Meditation was also popularized by the Beatles. Some of those in the ecology movement base their concern for the environment on the inherent "oneness" of the universe.[26] Man and nature are one in essence. Man is not much different from the animals. He is only higher on the great scale of being. The environment should be protected, not as a stewardship under God, but because we are all god, nature included.

The advance of Eastern thought was gradual, but layer by layer it gained acceptance. As Christianity steadily lost its hold on the heart and mind of the nation, softer forms of religious beliefs were more easily embraced. Christianity's drift into an emphasis on experience over objective, written revelation has made it easy prey for the pure subjectivism of Eastern thought. Robert J. L. Burrows, publications editor of the evangelical Spiritual Counterfeits Project in Berkeley, California, writes:

> Humans are essentially religious creatures, and they don't rest until they have some sort of answer to the fundamental questions. Rationalism and secularism don't answer those questions. But you can see the rise of the New Age as a barometer of the disintegration of American culture. Dostoevsky said anything is permissible if there is no God. But anything is also permissible if everything is God. There is no way of making any distinction between good and evil.[27]

Os Guinness wrote about the meeting of East and West in 1973, in what has become a standard Christian critique of the decline of secular humanism, *The Dust of Death*. He tells us that the "swing to the East has come at a time when Christianity is weak at just those points where it would need to be strong to withstand the East."[28] He goes on to show the three basic weaknesses within the Church that open it up to Eastern influences.

LEAPING INTO THE VOID

The first is its compromised, deficient understanding of revelation. Without biblical historicity and veracity behind the Word of God, theology can only grow closer to Hinduism. Second, the modern Christian is drastically weak in an unmediated, personal, experiential knowledge of God. Often what passes for religious experience is a communal emotion felt in church services, in meetings, in singing or contrived fellowship. Few Christians would know God on their own. Third, the modern church is often pathetically feeble in the expression of its focal principle of community. It has become the local social club, preaching shop or minister-dominated group. With these weaknesses, modern Christianity cannot hope to understand why people have turned to the East, let alone stand against the trend and offer an alternative.[29]

Western Christians have a faith that is "extremely blurred at the edges."[30] This opens them up to any and all spiritual counterfeits.

New Age humanism is anti-Christian to the core. It is a utopian dream built on a flawed understanding of man's nature and a devotion to a westernized Eastern philosophy in which God is nothing more than a cosmic Idea. The copy on the dust jacket to Ferguson's *The Aquarian Conspiracy* shows that the Christian's fears are justified: "A Leaderless but powerful network is working to bring about radical change in the United States. Its members have broken with certain key elements of Western thought, and they may even have broken with history." With all its seemingly "good" emphases, the New Age movement is at heart humanistic (man is the center of the universe), materialistic (self-actualization is all-important), and anti-God (the God of the Bible is dismissed in favor of self-deification). The American public, with its inability to distinguish Biblical truth from anti-Christian religious subtleties, is easily sucked in by the seemingly harmless religious and cultural goals of New Age humanism.

Our modern culture is a breeding ground for New Age concepts. New Age ideas are upbeat, optimistic, and seemingly life-transforming. At a time when you are most susceptible to change and influence, the New Age movement can be a dangerous "friend." Keep far from it.[31]

CULTURAL REBELLION

The 1960s are known for the great campus rebellion. While today's campus is somewhat more calm when compared to that tumultuous decade, the rebellion has moved back indoors. The classroom is where revolu-

Marxism

Perhaps you've heard the joke: There are no Marxists in the former Soviet Union because they all found professorships in American universities. Some joke! And it is not far from the truth. Though universities are not centers of revolutionary violence today as they were in the 1960s, Marxism is still alive and well on the university campus. Marxist scholarship is commonplace in literary studies, sociology, anthropology, and history. In some fields, Marxism and feminism are the *dominant* worldviews of scholars. Between 1970 and 1982, four Marxist textbooks in American government were published. In the 1960s, only a few universities taught courses on Marxism; today there are over 400 such courses at universities around the country.[32]

The Marxist professor is not always a raving lunatic revolutionary. Many sociologists and economists, for example, employ "Marxist analysis" without adopting wholesale its revolutionary agenda. But there are raving lunatics too. Harvard biologist Richard Lewontin has written in *New Political Science* that Marxism

> can do nothing *for* the university; the real question is what can Marxists do *to* and *in* the university. . . . For the natural and social scientist the answer is very clear. The university is a factory that makes weapons—ideological weapons—for class struggle, for class warfare, and trains people in their use. It has no other leading and important function in the social organization.[33]

In other words, some Marxist professors at least are at the university to train students to be revolutionaries. No wonder Secretary of Education William Bennett has warned about the prominence of antidemocratic opinion on the college campus.[34]

As mentioned above, Marxism has permeated many different areas of study. Don't think students are safe from Marxist influence by majoring in English literature. Marxist professors and concepts have infiltrated virtually every area of study.

What is the worldview of Marxism? It would be impossible to discuss every facet of Marxist thought in these few pages, so we will simply look at a few pertinent concepts.

LEAPING INTO THE VOID

1. *Marx viewed all religions, including Christianity, as illusions.* Despite recent efforts to reconcile Christianity with Marxism, atheism is a basic premise of the Marxist system of thought. Marx himself said that "man makes religion; religion does not make man," and concluded that religion is the "opium of the people," providing an illusion of happiness without true happiness.[35] Marxism, in short, is a materialistic worldview; the consistent Marxist believes that the material world is the ultimate reality, that there is no God beyond the forces of history and nature.

Significantly, Marx's main attack was not on the idea of God's existence as such, but on God's sovereign dominion over all things. He rejected the Christian doctrine of creation, because he realized that a Creator-God is also a Sovereign God. Marx's philosophical hero was the mythical character, Prometheus, whose battle cry was, "I hate all gods."[36]

2. *Marx's view of history, which has come to be known as "dialectical materialism," is consistent with his rejection of Christianity.* History is not the story of God's dealings with men, but the progress of man from one social arrangement to another, from feudalism to capitalism for example. This progress takes place through changes in technology that lead to changes in the way that people are organized for production. Changes in the organization for production in turn lead to ideological and political conflicts between those classes which want to conserve the old order and those which seek to make drastic changes. Revolutionary class conflict, whether peaceful or violent, produces social change.

In the history of the West, this process has caused the change from feudalism to capitalism, and will, Marx believed, cause the change from capitalism to "scientific" socialism. In the last stage of history, after a transitional stage of the "dictatorship of the proletariat" (lower urban classes), the State will wither and a classless society will emerge. The details are not as important here as the basic point that Marx viewed history as the unfolding of completely materialistic forces.

3. *Another key presupposition of Marx was his view of man.* As a materialist, Marx denied that each man is a creature made in the image of a sovereign God. Rather, man is an essentially social being, with no individual human nature. His whole life is bound up with his social relations. This did not mean for Marx that man has no control over his destiny, and in fact Marxism wavers between a deterministic view that socialism is inevitable, and the call to action. Man is determined by the social forces of history, but he can act to hasten the revolutionary change. This apparent contradiction is resolved by Marxism's ethical imperative for men to act in ways that correspond with the direction of history. The

ethical foundation of Marxism, in short, is to jump on the bandwagon that is moving in the direction of the revolution. The one ethical imperative in Marx is to "overthrow all relations in which man is a debased, enslaved, forsaken, despicable being," with the ultimate end being to restore man to his true humanity from which he is alienated by capitalist society. In other words, Marx sees his purpose as teaching that "man is the highest being for man."[37] The revolutionary social transformation from capitalism to socialism will produce a new man and a new human nature, no longer alienated from himself and nature.

What makes Marxism so appealing in culture today? First, it provides a comprehensive, positive vision of human life and history. Once Christianity is rejected, some other worldview will fill the void, and Marxism is a total worldview. Second, Marxism is particularly appealing because it offers an alternative to Christianity that is very similar in structure to Christianity. Like Christianity, Marxism teaches that history has meaning and direction. Like Christianity, Marxism teaches that man can be saved from his present condition of alienation. Like Christianity, Marxism looks forward to a complete transformation of society. Third, Marxism, in a simplified form, can be used as a weapon to attack opponents. Marx's claim that ideas are products of class has been used to undermine any and all philosophies. The Marxist radical can debunk a Christian's claim that God blesses His people by saying that the Christian view is just a product of a particular social class.

Liberation Theology

We have seen that Marxism is opposed to Christianity at several key points. It may surprise you, then, to discover that many Christians in this country and around the world believe that Christianity and Marxism are compatible. These "liberation theologians" advocate revolutionary social change as a legitimate goal of the church.

According to theologian Emilio A. Núñez, liberation theology is heavily indebted to Marxism.

> No one can fail to notice that Marxist thought exerts a powerful influence on liberation theology. And the exponents of liberation theology do not try to hide that influence. On the contrary, they seem to pride themselves on the use they make of Marxism both for social analysis and for the action they propose to transform the structures of Latin American society. Some of the

prominent ideas of liberation theology reveal Marxist influence: economics as a determining factor in the historical process, Marxist notions of work and class struggle, the liberating praxis of the oppressed by the oppressed themselves, man as a protagonist of his own history, the new man and the new society resulting from the proletarian revolution, as well as the ideological criticism of capitalism.[38]

What are the main features of liberation theology? Núñez lists several.

1. *Liberation theology says that an evangelical must be committed to overturning an unjust social system.* Sin is not merely a personal reality, but a social reality as well. The Christian helps to overturn an oppressive order by radically identifying himself with the poor and oppressed classes.

2. *Liberation theology's view of salvation is unbiblical in several key respects.* Núñez writes that "sin enters the picture, but the emphasis does not fall on individual sin but on social sin. Sin is characterized as an offense to one's neighbor, to the oppressed. There is no reference to the eternal consequences of sin, nor to the responsibility of the oppressed before the justice of God." Moreover, "not enough attention is given to the redemptive significance of the sacrifice of Christ, nor to the ministry of the Holy Spirit and the Word of God in the salvation of the sinner." Liberation theology does not stress the importance of repentance and faith, which are central to the biblical idea of salvation.[39]

3. *Liberation theologians often deny basic Christian doctrines, on such central issues as the person of Christ.* "Jesus of Nazareth, [liberation theology] claims, slowly became the Son of God; and the idea of the preexistent, eternal Word who came down from the Father to become a man in order to be the mediator between God and man is the product of theological development that took place after the resurrection of Christ."[40] In the writings he studied, Núñez found "no clear-cut, unambiguous confession that Jesus is God."[41]

4. *Liberation theology teaches that the mission of the church is not, as Jesus said, to "disciple the nations," but to "opt for the cause of the poor, to denounce the injustice of the oppressors, to announce the kingdom of God in order to 'conscientize' and 'politicize' the oppressed, and to participate directly in liberating praxis with a view toward establishing a socialist society that is 'more just, free, and human.'"*[42]

5. *Liberation theology, by making the feelings and experience of the oppressed masses the highest standard of theology and Christian practice,*[43] *replaces Scripture with the oppressed poor as the standard for action.*

There is no denying that the people of Latin America have been oppressed for centuries. But there are better solutions than the baptized Marxism of liberation theology. Marxism has never freed the poor from oppressors, and it will not do so in Latin America. Moreover, in many areas, as we have noted, liberation theology is at odds with orthodox Christianity. Because it uses Christian and biblical language, however, it is often difficult to see through the rhetoric. Also, liberation theology often plays on the guilt that many middle class Christians feel when they are confronted with the awful realities of Third World poverty and oppression. Liberation theology has made significant inroads into the evangelical world, so Christians must be on guard.

Feminism

Several years ago, a constitutional Amendment was proposed to equalize the relations between men and women. Known as the Equal Rights Amendment (ERA), it circulated throughout the United States for several years, with each state having an opportunity to vote for or against it. The ERA failed to get enough votes to become a constitutional amendment, but many writers have since noted that feminism has not been stopped by the defeat of the ERA. Instead, many of the main proposals of the radical feminists have been adopted as law. Feminism, in short, has triumphed, even as the ERA was being defeated. The feminist movement has been equally victorious in America's college classrooms.

A reporter at a recent meeting of the Modern Language Association in San Francisco observes that

> so prominent a part of the academic literary scene has feminism become that during one afternoon time slot at the convention no fewer than nine sessions on feminist topics from lesbian writing to "feminist dialogics" were droning on concurrently. Feminism has gone from being a special and rather narrow interest to having become one of the large clumsy categories by which literary study is organized in the university.[44]

Feminists have also infiltrated other areas of study, such as history, sociology, anthropology, and even theology.

Even some evangelical professors claim to be "biblical feminists." Virginia Ramey Mollenkott, who teaches English at William Paterson

LEAPING INTO THE VOID

College, calls herself an evangelical, but has co-authored a book advocating "covenantal homosexuality." At a meeting of the Evangelical Roundtable, she defended abortion, saying, "It is our right . . . it is our body . . . it is our choice."[45]

Within many mainline Christian denominations, a separate "feminist theology" has developed. One of the leading Roman Catholic feminists, Rosemary Radford Reuther, has proposed new liturgies for her "woman-church," including liturgies for healing after an abortion, covenanting of lesbian couples, and a Summer Solstice Party. Mary Jo Weaver, another Catholic feminist, asks what feminists can do about the traditional patriarchal church. She sees two possible alternatives: "to reject the tradition and search for new alternatives (usually focused on the Goddess and a revival of witchcraft) or to reinterpret the tradition in order to change its direction and open it to the influences and lives of women."[46] Some churches have changed their hymnals and Bibles to avoid masculine references to God, and some have gone so far as to place crucifixes in the church sanctuary with female Christs!

Some "feminist" historians are interested only in studying the place of women in history, and some "feminist" biblical scholars are only interested in understanding how the Bible addresses the problems of modern women. These are worthy exercises, and can be very fruitful. A study of President's wives, for example, can reveal a lot about American politics. But in addition to this relatively mild form of "feminism," there is a group of hard-core, self-conscious feminists whose main goal is to destroy the traditional family and Western "patriarchal" culture. At an extreme, there is a relatively small group of feminist witches. Though often scorned by other feminists, whose goals are mainly political, feminist witchcraft is the fastest growing segment of witchcraft in America today.[47]

What are the presuppositions of the feminist ideology?

1. *Radical feminists are virulently anti-Christian.* Some advocate a return to the ancient mythologies because the ancient pantheon of gods included female deities. Others do not go quite so far, but in the end, they have replaced the Christian God with woman. For the feminists, Woman is God. At a conference on woman's spirituality in 1976, the advent of the goddess was proclaimed. One feminist writer noted that "proclaiming that the 'Goddess is Alive' in a traditional church setting is proclaiming that . . . being female is divine."[48]

2. *Feminists seek equality for men and women.* Some seek more than this, desiring feminine dominance over men. But, even equality between men and women is not a legitimate goal for a Christian move-

ment. The Bible teaches that every institution in society has a structure of authority. There are elders in the church to rule the church; there are magistrates in the State to rule the citizens; and there are husbands who are to rule their families. Though the Bible does not teach men to tyrannize their wives, the Bible clearly states that men are to be heads of the home, and women are to submit to them (Ephesians 5:22-33). In seeking to overthrow this God-ordained order, radical feminists are simply rebelling against God. Rebellious tendencies are also manifested in the feminist advocacy of "unisex," in which an attempt is made to overcome God-ordained differences between the sexes.

3. *Feminism is often a form of Marxism.* The feminists see themselves as the oppressed and alienated sex, and their goal is to throw off the chains of oppression in order to liberate themselves. What they are seeking liberation from, of course, is the traditional family structure. They are also able to make the claims that Marxists do about the ideas of their opponents. Scholars who draw attention to the psychological and biological differences between men and women are dismissed because they are simply interested in maintaining the status quo. This tactic is often simply an attempt to dismiss evidence that is not consistent with the feminist outlook.

4. *These presuppositions of equality and liberation work out in a consistent social program.* As summarized by George Gilder, the ERA, if passed, would in all likelihood have had the following effects:

> 1) eliminated all rights of wives and mothers to be supported by their husbands, except to the extent husbands could claim an equal right; 2) eliminated all laws in any way restricting the rights of the gay liberation movement publicly to teach, proselytize, or practice their sexual ideology; 3) forced sexual integration of all schools, clubs, colleges, athletic teams, and facilities; 4) forced the drafting of women and the sexual integration of all military units; 5) threatened the tax exemption of most religious schools; and 6) compelled the use of government funds for abortions.[49]

Culture is also to be feminized. In fact, feminism has already made remarkable progress in transforming our culture into a feminist ideal. As one "biblical feminist" notes,

> Feminism since the early 1960s has begun to color interpersonal relations, the language we speak, family life, the educational sys-

tem, child-rearing practices, politics, business, the mass media, religion, law, the judicial system, the cultural values system, and intellectual life.⁵⁰

The feminist goal is nothing short of social, political, and cultural revolution.

The New Humanism

In the modern world, classical "humanism" has been in decline. Humanism in this context may be defined as the belief that man is an inherently dignified being, and that education in literature and history can produce men and women who are characterized by an appreciation of beauty and reason. The rise of modern technology and science, however, led many to see man as nothing more than a machine, while Darwin claimed that man was little more than an advanced ape. In the wake of two world wars, philosophies of despair became widespread as men were reminded again of their potential for evil. Man was seen as nothing more than a pawn in a meaningless sea of meaningless forces. Freud argued that men are controlled by subconscious appetites and drives. In all of these, man's dignity as the master of the world and the ability of his reason to discover meaning was called into question.

Recently, however, there has been a revival of the ancient and Renaissance idea of man as the "measure of all things," and of the ideal of a classical liberal education that will produce cultured and reasonable men and women. Secretary of Education under Ronald Reagan, William Bennett, for example, has outlined a new curriculum for the public schools. He proposed that school children be given a good dose of foreign languages, history, grammar, and literature. Similar proposals have been made for the university. In his surprise best-seller, University of Chicago professor Allan Bloom called for a return to the classical curriculum based on the "great books," particularly on Plato and Rousseau.⁵¹

Some of these "new humanists" trace their lineage back to the critical and cultural theories of Matthew Arnold, a nineteenth-century critic and poet. Arnold's great enemy was not sin, but "philistinism," the term he used to characterize vulgar middle-class culture and tastes. Unlike some of his contemporaries, Arnold did not turn toward the Middle Ages for values. He believed that England could never return to the Christian culture of that period, and insisted instead that men could lead good lives without any appeal to God or to revelation. In the place of the

"Hebraism" of the Middle Ages, Arnold proposed a return to Hellenism, to Greek thought and culture.

In his essay "Sweetness and Light," Arnold argued that the only hope for the future was a cult of beauty (sweetness) and reason (light).

> He who works for sweetness and light, works to make reason and the will of God prevail. . . . Culture has one great passion, the passion for sweetness and light . . . It is not satisfied till we all come to a perfect man; it knows that the sweetness and light of the few must be imperfect until the raw and unkindled masses of humanity are touched with sweetness and light.[52]

Good taste and the cultivation of reason are the goals of education. What all these "new humanists" leave out is, of course, the Bible. Arnold self-consciously rejected a return to Christianity as a viable alternative for Victorian England. Allan Bloom likewise believes that the Bible, while a source of truth, is only one source among many. And he places himself squarely in the Enlightenment tradition in education, in which "all things must be investigated and understood by reason."[53] Man, in this view, remains the measure of all things, and is not bound to submit himself to the Word of God. Though far less radical than the previous two worldviews, the new humanism is no less rebellious in principle.

The "new humanism" is less a consistent worldview than a philosophy of education. But as such it is likely to expand into the culture at large. The popularity of Bloom's book and the efforts of former Secretary of Education William Bennett make it likely that many colleges will begin to adopt this agenda. This is certainly preferable to the revolutionary scholarship of feminism and Marxism, but lacking a biblical foundation, this vision of education and society is ultimately doomed to failure.

Behaviorism

Behaviorism originated with the work of John B. Watson, an American psychologist. Watson claimed that psychology was not concerned with the mind or with human consciousness. Instead, psychology should be concerned only with behavior. In this way, men could be studied objectively, like rats and apes. Watson's work was based on the experiments of Ivan Pavlov, who had studied animals' responses to conditioning. In Pavlov's best-known experiment, he rang a bell as he fed some dogs several meals. Each time the dogs heard the bell they knew that a

LEAPING INTO THE VOID

meal was coming, and they would begin to salivate. Pavlov then rang the bell without bringing food, but the dogs still salivated. They had been "conditioned" to salivate at the sound of a bell. Pavlov believed, as Watson was later to emphasize, that humans react to stimuli in the same way.

Behaviorism is associated today with the name of B. F. Skinner, who made his reputation by testing Watson's theories in the laboratory. Skinner's studies led him to reject Watson's almost exclusive emphasis on reflexes and conditioning. People respond to their environment, he argued, but they also operate on the environment to produce certain consequences. Skinner developed the theory of "operant conditioning," the idea that we behave the way we do because this kind of behavior has had certain consequences in the past. For example, if your girlfriend gives you a kiss when you give her flowers, you will be likely to give her flowers when you want a kiss. You will be acting in expectation of a certain reward. Like Watson, however, Skinner denied that the mind or feelings play any part in determining behavior. Instead, our experience of reinforcements determines our behavior.

Behaviorism originated in the field of psychology, but it has had a much wider influence. Its concepts and methods are used in education, and many education courses at college are based on the same assumptions about man as behaviorism. Behaviorism has infiltrated sociology, in the form of sociobiology, the belief that moral values are rooted in biology. What are the presuppositions of behaviorism?

1. *Behaviorism is naturalistic.* This means that the material world is the ultimate reality, and everything can be explained in terms of natural laws. Man has no soul and no mind, only a brain that responds to external stimuli.

2. *Behaviorism teaches that man is nothing more than a machine that responds to conditioning.* One writer has summarized behaviorism in this way:

> The central tenet of behaviorism is that thoughts, feelings, and intentions, mental processes all, do not determine what we do. Our behavior is the product of our conditioning. We are biological machines and do not consciously act; rather we *react* to stimuli.[54]

The idea that men are "biological machines" whose minds do not have any influence on their actions is contrary to the biblical view that man is the very image of God—the image of a creative, planning, thinking God. In fact, Skinner goes so far as to say that the mind and mental processes are "metaphors and fictions" and that "behavior is simply part of the biology of the organism."[55] Skinner also recognizes that his view strips man of his "freedom and dignity," but insists that man as a spiritual being does not exist.

3. *Consistently, behaviorism teaches that we are not responsible for our actions.* If we are mere machines, without minds or souls, reacting to stimuli and operating on our environment to attain certain ends, then anything we do is inevitable. Sociobiology, a type of behaviorism, compares man to a computer: Garbage in, garbage out. This also conflicts with a Christian worldview. Our past experiences and our environment do affect the way we act, of course, but these factors cannot account for everything we do. The Bible teaches that we are basically *covenantal* creatures, not biological creatures. Our nearest environment is God Himself, and we respond most fundamentally to Him. We respond either in obedience to or rebellion against His Word.

4. *Behaviorism is manipulative.* It seeks not merely to understand human behavior, but to predict and control it. From his theories, Skinner developed the idea of "shaping." By controlling rewards and punishments, you can shape the behavior of another person. As a psychiatrist, one of Skinner's goals is to shape his patients' behavior so that he or she will react in more socially acceptable ways. Skinner is quite clear that his theories should be used to guide behavior:

> The experimental analysis of behavior has led to an effective technology, applicable to education, psychotherapy, and the design of cultural practices in general, which will be more effective when it is not competing with practices that have had the unwarranted support of mentalistic theories.[56]

In other words, Skinner wants behaviorism to be the basis for manipulating patients, students, and whole societies.

The obvious questions, of course, are: Who will use the tools? Who will pull the strings? Who will manipulate the technology? No doubt, Skinner would say that only someone trained in behavioral theory and practice would be qualified to "shape" the behavior of other persons. But this is contrary to the Biblical view, which commands us to *love* our neighbor, not to manipulate him.

In sum, the ethical consequences of behaviorism are great. Man is stripped of his responsibility, freedom, and dignity, and is reduced to a purely biological being, to be "shaped" by those who are able to use the tools of behaviorism effectively.

———————— LEAPING INTO THE VOID ————————

CONCLUSION

Naturalism was destined to fail. But it has left a number of disintegrating world views in its wake. These collapsing worldviews have sent thousands to look elsewhere for meaning. The lives of Charles Manson and his "Family" are tragic examples. But there are lessons in what happened. Manson appealed to the dregs of society, to those who were without hope. These "Family" members took a leap into the void of Manson's distorted world. What else could they do? Their spiritual craving had to be satisfied. In some twisted and perverted way, Charles Manson filled it.

> Most of the people at the ranch that you call the Family were just people that you did not want, people that were alongside the road, that their parents had kicked out, that did not want to go to Juvenile Hall. So I did the best I could and took them up on my garbage dump and I told them this: that in love there is no wrong.[57]

Manson's description of his worldview as a "garbage dump" is important. The naturalistic worldview led him and his followers into its logical consequence: If the world is all there is, then man must find meaning in himself. Manson "believe[ed] you could do no wrong, no bad. Everything was good. Whatever you do is what you are supposed to do; you are following your own karma."[58] Who can argue with such a premise? Only the Christian worldview has an answer.

6
SPIRITUAL COUNTERFEITS

> Every religious cult has two sets of differing creeds: the exoteric and the esoteric. The exoteric creed is the official, public doctrine, the creed which attracts the acolyte in the first place and brings him into the movement as a rank-and-file member. The esoteric creed is the unknown, hidden agenda, a creed which is only known to its full extent by the top leadership, the "high priests" of the cult. The latter are the keepers of the mysteries of the cult.[1]

FEW people find solace in the various worldview expressions of irrationalism. Many leave these bankrupt philosophies and return once again to Jesus Christ. But some turn to other forms of religions that often resemble Biblical Christianity. They are spiritual counterfeits, close to the originals but not close enough. Those who embrace cults will ultimately find disillusionment.

It's been said that "the cults are the unpaid bills of the church."[2] The vacuum caused by a retreating Christianity has made it possible for all types of spiritual counterfeits to invade our nation and capture the hearts and minds of the unsuspecting and vulnerable. The cults are one of the many options to which spiritual seekers turn when they are in need of spiritual vitality. But the surprising thing is that most cults cater to disenchanted church people. It seems that the cults offer what many churches have neglected. The spiritual vacuum must be filled. Unfortunately, many cult leaders are ready to seduce the broken hearted with a "different gospel" (Galatians 1:6).

What is a cult? Generally speaking, a cult is a religious movement that often claims support for its views by using the Bible but is fundamentally wrong on the basics of the Christian faith. To be more specific, a cult is any religious group which claims to be a more authentic expression of Christianity with its own distinctive interpretation on major doctrines. We know that not all Christians agree on every doctrine. But there are certain "core" doctrines that all Christians must believe in order to be called "Christian." Cults strike at the heart of these core doctrines.

WHAT TO LOOK FOR

Cults are not new to the Church, although most cults that we see today have not been around for more than a hundred years. While their contemporary expressions are new, their doctrinal distortions have been with us for centuries. Here's what to look for:

1. *There is more than one standard of authority.* Numerous cults have additional revelational books that are considered equal to the Bible in authority. Mormonism, for example, has the *Pearl of Great Price, Doctrine and Covenants, The Book of Mormon*, and continuing authoritative revelations by the "apostles" among the Mormon leadership. Other cults have an *interpreting* authority. While they might use the Bible and consider it to be authoritative, they believe that it takes a certain degree of spiritual discernment by a self-appointed or designated leader from the group to tell the members what the Bible *really* means. Sometimes books are designed by the hierarchy in the movement to be read along with the Bible. These books or "new revelations" become the interpreting code for the members to understand properly what God is saying. In time, the cult-produced books become the new authority.

Let's look at some of the cults and see how they misuse and reinterpret Biblical authority. The Jehovah's Witnesses have their own version of the Bible, *The New World Translation*, that obscures certain texts that are not compatible with their doctrines. This is most evident with those verses that teach the divinity of Christ. The Witnesses also determine doctrine by an unnamed hierarchy from the "Watchtower" organization. The Unification Church, whose members are often described as "Moonies" after its founder Sun Myung Moon, looks to Moon's *Divine Principle* to throw further light on the Bible: "It may be displeasing to religious believers, especially to Christians, to learn that a new expression of truth must appear. They believe in the Bible, which they now have, is perfect and absolute in itself." Christian Science has *Science and Health with Key to the Scriptures*. Mary Baker Eddy had this to say about the book's authority:

> I should blush to write of *Science and Health with Key to the Scriptures* as I have, were it of human origin and I apart from God its author, but as I was only a scribe echoing the harmonies of heaven in divine metaphysics, I can not be super-modest of the Christian Science Textbook.[3]

There are other groups that claim similar divine authority for their writings, prophecies, or doctrines: The Way International, The Children of God, Unity, Theosophy, Hare Krishna, and Scientology. You will probably encounter others. Your first question should be: "Is the Bible the only authority you have or must I look to some other book or a group of interpretations handed down from your leadership?" Of course, since cults are very deceptive, you may not get a straight answer.

2. *Jesus Christ is less than God, a great teacher, or a son of God just as we are all sons of God.* "Who do people say that the Son of Man is?" This was Jesus' question to His disciples. But Jesus went even further: "But who do *you* say I am?" This is the single most important question you can ask someone who seems a bit off concerning the basics of the Christian faith. The doctrine of the divinity of Christ, that Jesus is God in human flesh, is the single most important doctrine for the Christian Church. The divinity of Jesus separates Christianity from *all* other religions, philosophies, and cults.

Jesus is God in human flesh. He is not just *a* god or Michael the archangel (as the Jehovah's Witnesses teach), a pre-existent spirit, also the Father, one of many gods (as Mormons teach), a great moral teacher (as in most Eastern religions), a prophet (as in Islam), a reincarnated spiritual master (as in the New Age movement), or a son of God not much different from mankind in general (as probably most religious Americans who call themselves Christian believe). Some might go so far as saying that Jesus never existed. Or, if He did exist, then His life and deeds were manufactured by His disciples so they could start a new religious movement in His name. He is, therefore, the "ideal" for all of us to follow. This is the view of most theological liberals.

God became man in the person of Jesus Christ, the second Person of the Trinity (Godhead). This is why there are passages in the New Testament that refer to Jesus as a man. He was a man in the fullest sense of the word, except for one fallen human condition: sin. At the same time,

Jesus is God in the way the Father is God and the Spirit is God. "In the beginning was the Word [Jesus], and the Word was with God, and the Word was God.... And the Word became flesh, and dwelt among us, and we beheld His glory, glory as the only begotten from the Father, full of grace and truth" (John 1:1, 14). Here is a comparison chart to show how divine attributes are given to or claimed by Jesus:[4]

"THERE IS ONE GOD" (1 Corinthians 8:6)

GOD IS...	YAHWEH IS JESUS	...JESUS IS
Genesis 1:1 Job 33:4 Isaiah 40:28	CREATOR	John 1:1-3 Colossians 1:12-17 Hebrews 1:8-12
Isaiah 41:4 Isaiah 44:6 Isaiah 48:12	FIRST & LAST	Revelation 1:17 Revelation 2:8 Revelation 22:13
Exodus 3:13, 14 Deuteronomy 32:39 Isaiah 43:10	I AM (EGO EIMI)	John 8:24, 58 John 13:19 John 18:5
Genesis 18:25 Psalm 96:13 Joel 3:12	JUDGE	2 Timothy 4:1 2 Corinthians 5:10 Romans 14:10-12
Psalm 47 Isaiah 44:6-8 Jeremiah 10:10	KING	Matthew 2:1-6 John 19:21 1 Timothy 6:13-16
Psalm 27:1 Isaiah 60:20	LIGHT	John 1:9 John 8:12
Psalm 106:21 Isaiah 43:3, 11 Isaiah 45:21-23	SAVIOR	John 4:42 Acts 4:10-12 1 John 4:14
Psalm 23 Psalm 100:3 Isaiah 40:11	SHEPHERD	John 10:11 Hebrews 13:20 1 Peter 5:4

In Israel, the worship of any god other than Jehovah brought with it the death penalty. So then, for Jesus to accept worship if He were not indeed God would mean that He was either a lunatic or a deceiver. If Jesus believed Himself to be God and was mistaken, then He was insane. He certainly would not be worthy of our worship. If Jesus misled the people into believing that He was God, then He is no more than a con artist who deserves our scorn. But if He is what He said He was, then He deserves our worship.

Neither men nor angels are to be worshipped, and yet Jesus willingly accepted worship. In Revelation 19:10 an angel refuses worship from the Apostle John: "Do not do that; I am a fellow servant of yours and your brethren who hold the testimony of Jesus; worship God." A similar incident occurs in Revelation 22:9. In Acts 10:25-26, Peter refuses worship from Cornelius. In Acts 14:11-15, Paul and Barnabas refuse worship at Lystra.

But notice the difference when it comes to the worship of Jesus. First, the wise men came to worship Him: "Where is He who has been born King of the Jews? For we saw His star in the East, *and have come to worship Him*. . . . And they came into the house and saw the child with Mary His mother; *and they fell down and worshipped Him*" (Matthew 2:2, 11). At that point Mary could have said: "Wait! He is no more than a man."

Second, Jesus accepted worship from others and did not rebuke those who came to worship Him: "And behold, Jesus met them and greeted them. And they came up and took hold of His feet *and worshipped Him*" (Matthew 28:9).

Third, Jesus accepted the title of "Lord and God": "Thomas answered and said to [Jesus], 'My Lord and my God!' " (John 20:28). Jesus' response was far different from that of Peter, Barnabas, and the angel in the book of Revelation: "Because you have seen Me, have you believed? Blessed are they who did not see, and yet believed" (v. 29). There is no rebuke for Thomas. Jesus accepted the titles "Lord and God."

The Christian faith revolves around the doctrine of Jesus' divinity. All cults distort this fundamental doctrine and turn Jesus into something less than God in human flesh.

3. *There is the need for a new interpretation of what true Christianity is all about.* Cults usually begin through the leadership of an individual who has become disenchanted with some aspect of Biblical Christianity and now presents his system as the "true" interpretation of the faith. An example of this is found in the writings of Herbert W. Armstrong, founder of the Worldwide Church of God:

> I found that the popular church teachings and practices were not based on the Bible. They had originated, as research in history had revealed, in paganism. Numerous Bible prophecies foretold it; the amazing unbelievable truth was, the SOURCE of these popular beliefs and practices of professing Christianity, was

quite largely paganism, and human reasoning and custom, NOT the Bible![5]

What is Armstrong's "truth" as opposed to these "popular church teachings and practices"? First, the gospel message of Jesus' saving work has not been preached since A.D. 69. It has only been since Herbert W. Armstrong's resurrection of the gospel that we have had the truth. Second, there is more than one God. God is a "family" that is open to others to join. This teaching is similar to that of Mormonism and some branches of eastern mysticism and the New Age movement. Third, the destiny of man is to become God. Armstrong says, "You are setting out on a training to become creator—to become God!" Fourth, man is saved by his own "good works." According to Armstrongism, "People have been taught, falsely, that 'Christ completed the plan of salvation on the cross'—when actually it was only begun there." Of course, it's for us to finish by our own supposed good works. These are the doctrines that have been hidden for nearly two thousand years.

People who talk this way are usually pushing a cult, whether old or new. Here's a list of some cults and their leaders:

Christian Science—Mary Baker Eddy
Jehovah's Witnesses—Charles Taze Russell
Mormonism—Joseph Smith
The Way International—Victor Paul Wierwille
The Unification Church—Sun Myung Moon
The Children of God—David Brandt Berg
The Worldwide Church of God—Herbert W. Armstrong
Unity—Charles Sherlock Fillmore
Forum (formerly known as est)—Werner Erhard

People looking for answers are often convinced by these admittedly charismatic figures. They appeal to the dissatisfaction that some may feel about their waning spiritual vitality. Many people are seduced because their circumstances have made them vulnerable: loss of a loved one in death, divorce, dissatisfaction with their present church, loneliness, or the unfulfillment of any number of heart-felt needs. People are vulnerable to the appeals of the cults if they are spiritually insecure. Believing that their churches are not meeting their emotional, intellectual, or spiritual needs, many people look outside traditional Christian denominations for fulfillment. They often discover that the tightly-knit fellowship of a cult is emotionally satisfying. They are looking for answers and this leader seems to have them.

The best antidote to seduction is a thorough knowledge of Scripture, knowing what you believe and why, and a strong church where the Word of God is preached faithfully and your spiritual needs can be met. The best way to spot a counterfeit is to be familiar with the original.

4. *Salvation is gained by good works.* If there is a new or twisted authority and a different Jesus, then we should expect a different gospel.

> I am amazed that you are so quickly deserting Him who called you by the grace of Christ, for a different gospel; which is really not another; only there are some who are disturbing you, and want to distort the gospel of Christ. But even though we, or an angel from heaven, should preach to you a gospel contrary to that which we have preached to you, let him be accursed (Galatians 1:6-8).

There is no grace in the cults, only works. What Jesus did on the cross was not enough. We have to add our good works to His less than sufficient sacrifice. What question should you ask of a cult evangelist?: "What must I do to be saved?" If he tells you anything more than "Believe on the Lord Jesus Christ," then it's time to bring *him* the true meaning of redemption.

Salvation by works is the most common doctrine the cults use to deny the sufficiency of Christ's death. But there are variations:

- *Salvation by faith in the leader of the cult.* Jim Jones of the Guyana tragedy became the focus of salvation. He was called "Father." Jesus may be important to these cultists, but He is still not enough. Charles Manson, while he did not create a new cult that gained wide acceptance, did structure his "Family" along cultic lines. One Manson cult member said this about him: "He represented a God to me that was so beautiful that I'd do anything for him."[6]

- *Salvation through "god-consciousness."* This type of salvation is found in most cults with an Eastern flavor such as the Unification Church or "Moonies." But it is also found in Christian Science. For Christian Scientists, the world is an "illusion." (In Hinduism, a similar concept is described by the world *maya*.) "Hence, evil is but an illusion, and it has no real basis. Evil is a false belief."[7] The New Age movement stresses god-consciousness. For all these groups, god-consciousness is very subjective.

Some Additional Cult Characteristics

The four pillars discussed above are found in all cults to one degree or another. But there are additional peculiarities that show up in the more extreme cults. Keep in mind that not all cults will manifest these characteristics. Some of them will only be exhibited in lesser degrees and may not be immediately obvious to a prospective cult member:

• An elite membership: "God has chosen us by giving us the truth. All other groups are wrong. Only our way is right."

• Demand to break family relationships: "We are your true family. You must forsake your earthly father and mother. Our leader is your new father."

• Surrender of possessions: "If you are truly committed to God's plan for your life, you must be willing to turn your possessions over to God's chosen leader."

• A change in daily routine: "You must work on a daily basis to prove your faithfulness to your religious commitment. This will mean witnessing, raising money, and avoiding contacts with family and friends. You will have to stop eating meat since we believe all life is sacred."

• Threat of losing your "salvation" if you leave the group: "If you leave the true religion, there will be no hope for you either in life or death. You will lose your salvation."

• Doctrinal ambiguity: "Well, you are not ready to understand our doctrines. Don't question new concepts. You are just a beginner. You must trust our leader. Your thoughts don't count. Do not trust your mind, your thinking processes."

• Scripture twisting: "You were taught, 'Blessed are the pure in heart, for you shall see God.' While this is true, there is more: 'Yes, blessed are those who purify their consciousness, for they shall see themselves as God.'"

• A corrupt leadership: "You should not question the actions of our leader. He is far above us. He is much better than we."

• The destruction of individuality: "We must be like our leader so we must give up our individuality, our personal desires, even our possessions. Even our children must be like him."

• Control of incoming information: "We can't allow you to have contact with those outside. They might influence you with the things of the world."

SPIRITUAL COUNTERFEITS

PSYCHOLOGICAL SEDUCTION

Many cults take advantage of young people who seem to be confused about life. Some cults use psychological techniques to gain the confidence of skeptics. Instead of arguing with newcomers about doctrine, the cultists might turn to proven psychological techniques that work to fulfill a person's physical, psychological, social, or spiritual needs that are not being met anywhere else. This could include some of the following:

1. "Love Bombing": Many cults shower prospective members with an inordinate amount of attention and affection. From the moment a person enters a meeting, he will be assigned a "chaperon" to give him constant attention. This technique is designed to break down any barriers of resistance a person might have erected when he agreed to come to a meeting.

2. Information Overload: Cultists know that they must break down certain preconceived ideas that young people have about the world in general and religion in particular. They also know that most Christians do not know much about the "whys" of their faith. They prey on ignorance. In order to short-circuit a prospect's belief system, he may be subjected to confusing lectures filled with the cult's favorite doctrines, the failure of all Christian movements, and Scripture passages quoted out of context. In time, it all might "make sense."

3. Meaningless Activities: Cultists must keep prospective converts from thinking about the new information that they hear. Cult leaders know that much of what they will tell a prospective cult member is radically different from what he or she has been raised on. In order to keep the prospects from questioning the new information, they often will be kept busy by the leadership until the next overload session of information occurs.

4. Group Bonding: Some cults design techniques to "bond" potential members to the group and to the leader. A student may be asked (compelled) to join in a group game where she is at the center of attention and the group supports her psychologically, emotionally, and physically. This might mean trusting yourself to the group by falling back into the arms of a cult member. From an experience like this you will learn to depend on and trust the group more than your friends or family.

THE END OF THE WORLD LURE

Some cults entice prospective members by spinning a scenario that includes the near end of the world and the return of Christ in judgment. The Jehovah's Witnesses have made this a part of their "evangelistic" strategy since 1914. Converts are attracted to cults that maintain that Jesus is coming back on a certain day, and by joining with them, the bearers of the only true religion, they can avoid the impending judgment that will consume everyone else. Here's an extreme example:

> The group known as "The Lighthouse Gospel Tract Foundation," led by Bill Maupin, was located in Tucson. He originally calculated that the Rapture would take place on June 28, 1981. Some members of the group quit their jobs and/or sold their houses. When that date passed, Maupin said that he had miscalculated by forty days, and predicted that the Rapture would take place on August 7, 1981. The Return of Christ is to occur May 14, 1988. Maupin calculated his dates on the basis of Daniel's seventy "weeks," and the founding of the State of Israel on May 15, 1948.[8]

The important thing to pick up on in the above quotation is that they "quit their jobs and/or sold their houses." I've heard of students who joined similar cults and dropped out of school in anticipation of "the end." The Children of God began as a somewhat fundamentalist sect, but later turned into a doomsday cult. They believed that the end of the world was just around the corner. Their leader, David Berg, had had visions supporting the claim. Acting on their belief, the cult members embraced an itinerant lifestyle and lived in the shadow of Christ's soon coming.

New cults come on the scene without warning. Be very careful of the seemingly orthodox religious groups that tell you it knows when Jesus is going to return. Well-intentioned but mistaken prophetic speculators have been with us since the second century A.D., all of whom have been wrong in their predictions about when Jesus Christ will return.

CONCLUSION

The cults are Christian counterfeits. What is a counterfeit? A counterfeit is an illicit copy of an original designed to be passed off as the real thing. You're most familiar with the counterfeiting of United States currency. The important thing to remember about counterfeiting is that there is a genuine article that is being copied. If there is no genuine article, then there can be no counterfeit. If someone handed you a three dollar bill, you would know immediately that it wasn't real. You might, however, be hard pressed to spot a counterfeit ten dollar bill.

SPIRITUAL COUNTERFEITS

We do not often consider "theological counterfeiting" as a way the devil might hide the truth from Bible-believing Christians. Yet the Bible shows us that there are counterfeit Christs (Matthew 24:5; Acts 5:36, 37), counterfeit prophets (Matthew 7:15; 24:11), counterfeit miracles (Exodus 7:8-13), counterfeit angels (2 Corinthians 11:14), counterfeit gods (Galatians 4:8; Acts 12:20-23), counterfeit good works (Matthew 7:15-23), counterfeit converts and disciples (1 John 2:19), counterfeit spirits (1 John 4:1-3), counterfeit doctrines (1 Timothy 4:3), counterfeit kings (John 19:15), counterfeit names (Revelation 13:11-18; cf. 14:1), counterfeit gospels (Galatians 1:6-10), counterfeit kingdoms (Daniel 2; Matthew 4:8-11; Acts 17:1-9), and a counterfeit new age (Revelation 13:11-18). Cults are counterfeits. They want the *fruit* of Christianity without the *root*.

7
THE OCCULT EXPLOSION

> There are two equal and opposite
> errors into which our race can fall
> about the devils. One is to disbelieve
> in their existence. The other is to
> believe, and to feel an excessive and
> unhealthy interest in them. They
> themselves are equally pleased by both
> errors and hail a materialist or a
> magician with the same delight.[1]

WHO would have thought that the devil would still be popular as we near the end of the twentieth century, especially in the light of the reason-alone, rationalistic worldview that prevails in our nation? Well, he is. Even the non-Christian craves the supernatural. "Theologian Protests 'Witchcraft at Indiana University'" is the title of a newspaper article that denounces the way college students are being duped by the supposed "reasonableness" of witchcraft. It seems that witchcraft is "better for women than Christianity." "Ms. Budapest," a self-proclaimed witch who claims to be descended from an eight hundred-year-old line of witches, presented a lecture on "Religion, Women, and Power." The professor who invited "Ms. Budapest" to speak is also a witch.[2]

Devil worship is showing up in criminal cases. Signs of it appeared in the serial killings committed in Los Angeles by the suspected "Night Stalker," Richard Ramirez. At one point during his trial, he left the courtroom shouting "Hail Satan!" The death of a fifteen-year-old girl has been linked to the occult. A sheriff from Douglas County, Georgia, "said the suspects' motives in the killing involved sex, satanic devil worship and witchcraft. 'To a certain extent, I know they are involved in (devil worship). There's a good possibility that a portion of the motive has to do with sex, and additionally the motive has to do with devil-worshipping and witchcraft.'"[3]

Some cases of child abuse are being linked to "ritual abuse." Dr. Gregory Simpson, a Los Angeles pediatrician, began looking into the ritual abuse of children in 1985 as a result of seeing ritual scarring on patients. "One dead girl's chest was carved with a pentagram, he says. 'The conclusion I reached is that satanic abuse of small children does exist, and it's something that needs to be dealt with by the medical community.'"[4]

Investigative journalist and author Maury Terry believes the "Son of Sam" killings that terrorized New York City in 1977 involved Satanists. Similar suspicions arose during the trial of Charles Manson and his followers. The police no longer dismiss Satanism when they uncover what look like ritualistic murders like those in the "Night Stalker" case. Ramirez was fond of painting pentagrams, a favorite satanic symbol, in the homes of his victims.

Drugs, hypnosis, sexual abuse, brainwashing techniques, and intimidation are used to bring children and occult initiates under the control of the Satanists. Those who escape from satanic movements are often hunted down by members of the group. What "theology" do these members encounter that makes it so attractive? Patricia Pulling, founder of B.A.D.D. (Bothered About Dungeons and Dragons), an organization based in Richmond, Virginia, that seeks to educate young people about baneful influences, describes the perverted worldview of the occult:

> The satanists' theology derives in a perverted fashion from the Old Testament description of God as a jealous god—jealous, in particular, of Satan, says Pulling. If God and Satan are on equal planes and their battle is eternal, as satanists believe, why take the side of God, who places restrictions on what man may do? Why not take the side of Satan, who will help you satisfy your desires? Why try to deny the appetites that arise from the sin you are born into?[5]

The devil has become God's cosmic equal. Why believe in a God who restricts sinful desires when you can worship the devil and have all your desires met? This form of Satanism grows out of irrationalism, in which all things are possible, and monism, in which "all is god." There is also a sprinkling of Manichaeanism, an ancient philosophy in which the principles of Evil (Darkness and Matter) and Good (Spirit and Light) are deified. This view enabled Charles Manson to combine without conflict both Christ and Satan in himself.

THE TURNING POINT

There have always been movies with the devil as part of the plot. *Angel on My Shoulder* (1946) and *The Devil and Daniel Webster* (1941) are two of the best. *The Devil and Daniel Webster* is a sometimes comedic but always authentic portrayal of the devil and his schemes. It's reminiscent of C. S. Lewis' immortal *Screwtape Letters*. A simple, down-and-out farmer sells his soul to the devil in exchange for riches. In the end, the farmer changes his mind and turns to the great nineteenth-century orator and lawyer Daniel Webster to get him out of the contract. A jury of long-dead scoundrels, who had likewise sold their souls, is called up from the pit of hell to sit in judgment. After hearing the pleading by Webster, they allow the seemingly doomed farmer to break his former contract with "Scratch," the devil's apprentice who originally beguiled the farmer.

The devil had been trivialized in Walt Disney's 1937 first animated feature, *Snow White*, and the screen adaptation of Frank Baum's *Wizard of Oz* continued the trivialization process. "The influence of Walt Disney's witch in the animated movie, *Snow White*, while terrifying to young children, is amusing to adults. To a great extent, this is the traditional image of the witch: broomstick, black hat, black cat near at hand. It is as old as the medieval witchcraft trials."[6] The American public would soon be caught off guard by the new devil of special effects and a revived occultism.

Something happened at the movies beginning in the sixties. Prior to this time, the devil always knew his place. He was a defeated and doomed creature whose power was limited. He was real but under control. But today, the devil is no longer so accommodating. First, there was *Rosemary's Baby* (1968).[7] An overly ambitious actor "sells" his wife to a cult of devil-worshipers so he can gain fame and fortune. Why do these Satanists want her? You might have guessed: Mia Farrow, who plays the actor's wife, Rosemary, is raped by Satan in order to bring his child into the world. How does it end?: Rosemary grows to love her "demon seed." By the way, *Demon Seed* is the title of another occult "classic." A super-computer named "Proteus" (a god noted for his ability to assume different forms) mates with the wife of a computer scientist. The devil has entered the world of "high tech."

Then came *The Exorcist* in 1973. In this blockbuster movie the devil seems to get the upper hand again. The movie ends with the devil leaving the possessed girl, only to enter and destroy the exorcist. After seeing Father Karras hurl himself out the window in an act of desperation, the audience is left with the impression that the devil won the battle.

In the occult movie *The Omen*, a 1976 box office hit, the devil is incarnated in the form of a five-year-old boy sired by the devil himself, and adopted by a wealthy American couple which was unaware of his origin. *The Omen* spawned two sequels, *Damien—The Omen II* (1978) and *The Final Conflict* (1981). In these movies Satan made a comeback—but as a different devil. No longer was he a submissive creature condemned to judgment. He was now an equal with God Himself. God seemed to be absent from the universe, or at least helpless to do anything.

Why the revival of the devil and the demonic at this point in history? And why his new status as God's equal? The devil has always had to be reckoned with. In the Christian worldview he was tempter, adversary, and accuser, but he always operated under the sovereignty of God (Job 1:6-22). He was always considered to be under God's control. Christians rarely believed that he had the upper hand. The Bible says that Satan is defeated, disarmed, and spoiled (Colossians 2:15; Revelation 12:7ff.; Mark 3:27), "fallen" (Luke 10:18), and "thrown down" (Revelation 12:9). He was "crushed" under the feet of the early Christians (Romans 16:20). He has lost "authority" over Christians (Colossians 1:13) and has been "judged" (John 16:11). He cannot "touch" a Christian (1 John 5:18). His works have been "destroyed" (1 John 3:8). He has "nothing" (John 14:30). He "flees" when "resisted" (James 4:7) and is "bound" (Mark 3:27; Luke 11:20).

Then something happened. The Christian message began to wane. The devil was seen as the one in control. Supposedly he rules the earth until Jesus returns to set up His earthly kingdom. Satan is considered to be "alive and well on planet earth" while God seems "to be holed up in his corner of the universe sulking,"[8] unable to lift a finger to stop the devil. Add to this the reduction of Christianity, the demise of rationalism, the rise of irrationalism, and the popularity of monism, and you have a volatile mix. There are those who will try anything to find fulfillment. Unfortunately, the occult is no longer off-limits.

Beyond Good and Evil

For the monist, good and evil are beyond this world. All is One. There are no ethical or moral distinctions in the One and no differentiation in being; that is, you are just as much a god as anyone else, and there is no god over you. The spiritual seeker must transcend the world of illusion and enter the world of unity with the One. "All actions are merely part of the whole world of illusion. The only 'real' reality is ultimate reality, and that is beyond differentiation, beyond good and evil. . . . So, like true and false, ultimately the category of good and evil fades away. Everything is good (which, of course, is identical to saying, 'Nothing is good' or 'Everything is evil')."[9] Tampering with evil in monism is no real problem since evil is no longer a category with ethical content.

So then, rationalism and monism are dangerous on two fronts. First, rationalism would have us dismiss the demonic, the world of spirits, and occult realities. Second, monism opens us to an unhealthy interest in the occult. In nearly all Eastern religions, there is open idolatry, superstition, animism (the belief that spirits inhabit objects), and spiritism.

OCCULTISM: PLAYING WITH FIRE

Occultism emerges in a society when the prevailing Christian worldview fails to impact people's lives by refusing to address the issues of life with concrete, life-transforming answers. When the Christian message becomes defeatist, retreatist, and otherworldly, the door is open wide to the occult. Occultism, then, prospers when Christianity is reduced. When the Church embraces a truncated Christian message and raises the white flag of cultural surrender, you can expect the devil to march in where he once feared to tread.[10] Os Guinness writes:

> Early hunters on safari in Africa used to build their fires high at night in order to keep away the animals in the bush. But when the fires burned low in the early hours of the morning, they would see all around them the approaching outlined shapes of animals and a ring of encircling eyes in the darkness. When the fire was high they were far off, but when the fire was low they approached again.[11]

We see that the encircling eyes of the occult are all around us because the Church has allowed the fires of a vibrant Christian faith to burn low. What were the steps of the ruin of Christianity and the rise of the occult?

First, a large segment of the Church "demythologized" the Bible. Anything that could not be explained rationally was discarded as myth.

Today, this view prevails in most colleges and many seminaries. The belief in the devil is counted as an old-world superstition that has no modern-day validity.

Second, the Bible itself is no longer considered authoritative. The Bible is presumed to be riddled with errors. Supposedly it is true only on matters dealing with "faith," that is, how to get to heaven and live a quiet life until Jesus returns. Many conservative Christians hold this view of the Bible. For them, Scripture does not address political, economic, educational, and legal issues, and is not considered reliable when it mentions a personal devil. For these anti-supernaturalists, there is no devil. The Bible used the devil only to enhance the story of Jesus' conflict between good and evil. While Jesus may have believed in the devil, He was just a man of the times. He was susceptible to all the then current superstitions. All this has had the effect of discrediting the Bible. Without an authoritative standard like the Bible to define truth and error, good and evil, and right and wrong, experience has became the norm, and the occult offers just one experience among many.

Third, the Christian message was diluted in its effect in and on this world. An otherworldly-only gospel was adopted: The Bible has answers in death but little to say in life. Those looking for answers to daily problems will try any option, including the occult. Many supposedly Bible-believing Christians refuse to turn to Scripture in any systematic and consistent way to deal with contemporary issues such as poverty, crime, education, and politics. For them, the Bible is a "spiritual," otherworldly book that should only be consulted for the latest in prophecy. What Jesus meant in John 18:36 when he told Pilate that His kingdom was not "of this world," was that His kingdom did not operate *in* and *over* this world.

Fourth, paganism, which supposedly has received a "bum rap" from Christianity and the scientific community (for different reasons), is now seen as a viable worldview option. Once the Bible is dismissed as authoritative on everything on which it speaks (and it speaks on everything),[12] we are left with a free-for-all when it comes to a choice of worldviews. The worldview of relativism makes all other worldviews possible and permissible. Witchcraft thrives in a relativistic world where Christianity is only one religious alternative among many, as the following quotation makes crystal clear:

> One need not be a witch—I am not—to understand witchcraft as a valid expression of the religious experience. The religion of witchcraft offers to restore a lost option, paganism, to our reli-

THE OCCULT EXPLOSION

gious worldview. Both Christianity and scientism have taught us falsely that paganism is nonsense. We are taught that pagans worshipped idols, that they believed undignified things about a useless variety of silly gods, and that they invented interesting but irrelevant myths. . . . The religions of Egypt and Canaan, of the Celts and the Teutons, when properly understood, are rich, sophisticated, beautiful, and psychologically full of insight. The neopagan witches are attempting to recreate the positive values of pagan religion.[13]

The man-centered worldview of rationalism and the truncated worldview of Christianity produced a new worldview which is now being identified as the New Age movement, higher consciousness, holistic healing, psychic healing, astrology, eastern mysticism, life readings, and outright Satanism.

IRRATIONALISM'S OPEN DOOR TO THE OCCULT

But doesn't it seem rather strange that with the collapse of Christian belief we should see a revival of the occult? Not too long ago Christians were ridiculed for believing in witchcraft. John Wesley wrote: "The giving up of witchcraft is in effect giving up of the Bible." The noted atheist Bertrand Russell nastily added, "I think he was right."[14] Ah, but the giving up of the Bible by Russell and others has turned the devil loose on the world. Today's devil is far more sinister. Rationalism declared that witchcraft, the devil, and a power-inducing occult were dead. But rationalism has been steadily losing its grip on certainty. The world is now up for grabs, and belief in the devil is just another brass ring. "The door to the non-rational, the irrational and super-rational is wide open. One of the many previous 'unthinkables' which has squeezed through the door is the occult."[15]

"POP" OCCULTISM

Many people are introduced to the occult through seemingly harmless practices, such as seances, Ouija boards, astrology, and *Dungeons & Dragons*. This is "pop occultism." At first, there is little that seems sinister. In fact, it seems like fun. It's a way "to escape from a drab and burdensome life."[16] Let's look at a few of the open doors that can lead to the acceptance of the occult as an acceptable worldview.

Astrology

Instead of seeking answers to life's problems in the Bible, millions of Americans turn to the stars each day to search for spiritual direction. There are over two thousand newspapers in the United States that carry a daily horoscope. Jeanne Dixon and other astrologers have a daily telephone horoscope. Just dial a number and get instant direction for your life. Astrology plays a major role in the lives of millions around the world. The Bible is no longer God's Word to man, and if it is, it's not enough. It's surprising how many Christians are horoscope readers. Millions of Americans (some estimate 32 million) are willing to trust their lives to the impersonal movements of the stars rather than a God who gives specific direction in the Bible.[17]

Astrology is also very irrational. You can't be born under a particular "sign." All the supposed "signs" are made out of non-patterned star points. It's like "connect the dots" with more dots than you need. You can then turn any group of stars into any sign you want. Find a book on constellations, choose the constellations Leo and Cancer, redraw the stars as points on a blank sheet of paper, and then hand the paper to a friend and have him connect the dots in the form of a lion (Leo) and crab (Cancer). Then ask someone else to connect the dots to look like two other animals. What's the point? The dots can be made to look like anything you want. The astrological signs are arbitrary renderings.

Then there is the problem of alignment. At your particular moment of birth, the sun, planets, and stars are in a particular alignment. But are they really? Light from the sun takes 8.3 light-*minutes*. This means that light from the sun, traveling one hundred eighty-six thousand miles per second takes more than eight minutes to reach Earth. Jupiter is nearly 51 light-minutes away from Earth, and Pluto 5.6 light-*hours*. This means that when you see the sun you are actually seeing what happened eight minutes before you actually see it. The closest stars are measured in light-*years*. None of these heavenly bodies are aligned in the way you see them. A planet has shifted position a number of times before you even see the light from a distant star.

The Ouija Board

The Ouija board is another pop occult "game." Thousands of children each year place their hands on a device that mysteriously travels across the face of the board, either spelling out words or simply

THE OCCULT EXPLOSION

answering yes or no to questions asked of it. But who or what is doing the answering? Is it possible to go further into the occult through this seemingly harmless game? Some people think so. The use of the Ouija board "suggests communication with a nonmaterial world, a world of ghosts and disembodied waves . . . a yearning toward contact with unknown powers, a seeking for what has been called the Unexplained."[18] Playing with the Ouija board can make the spiritual seeker a bit more inquisitive about the powers of the occult.

Dungeons & Dragons

Some enter the occult world through a seemingly harmless game called *Dungeons & Dragons*. The "game" is sold through toy stores as "fun and fantasy." Players compete to "summon demons to defeat opponents" and to "employ dark forces to win battles." Games are also used in classes for "gifted" children in some public schools. The games have been up-dated to include electronic versions to be used with computers.

> The motifs of FRPs [Fantasy Role Playing] are reinforced by other aspects of youth culture. Saturday morning cartoons feature the *Masters of the Universe*, muscle-bound barbarians living in a world of magicians, witches, and sorcerers. You can get *Masters of the Universe* dolls, balls, comic books, and videos. There's even a feminist version: *She-Ra, Princess of Power*.[19]

What harm can these games do? Well, they initially trivialize the occult by calling *Dungeons & Dragons* a "game." Remember the quotation that introduced this chapter? C. S. Lewis warned us about refusing to believe in the existence of devils or feeling "an excessive and unhealthy interest in them." *Dungeons & Dragons* moves a person from disbelief ("it's only a game") to an unhealthy interest ("an incredible sense of power"). A frustrated writer admitted that he had experienced "an incredible sense of power" as a Dungeon Master. "In some games," he acknowledged, "they don't call me Dungeon Master; they call me God."[20]

Now, not everyone who toys with astrology, the Ouija board, and *Dungeons & Dragons* becomes an occultist. My point is that they can open the door to an unhealthy interest in things that are not good to fool with.

THE BIBLE AND THE OCCULT

What is the "occult" and how can you spot occult practices? The word "occult" is derived from the Latin word *occultus*, and it conveys the idea of things hidden, secret, or mysterious. You should keep in mind that involvement in the occult is often very subtle. Many people may not know that they have been seduced by occult teachings. Of course, this is what seduction is all about. "Under the designation occult we could class at least the following items: witchcraft, magic, palm reading, fortune telling, ouija boards, tarot cards, satanism, spiritism, demons and the use of crystal balls."[21] To this list we could add astrology, Dungeons & Dragons, seances, preoccupation with UFOs, Masonry, astral projection, hypnotism, mind reading, ESP, life readings, psychic healing, the sorcery techniques and philosophy of Carlos Casteneda, and the New Age movement.

The purpose of the occult is to get around God's way of dealing with the world. In all occult techniques, the practitioner either wants something that God forbids or pursues a good thing contrary to God's expressed will. God wants things done His way. Man, as the perpetual rebel, believes that he can subvert God's moral order by going to a lesser self-appointed god, Satan. But even Satan exacts a price: Adam and Eve lost Paradise (Genesis 2:15-17; 3:5, 14-24), Saul lost his kingdom (1 Samuel 28:3-19), and Judas most certainly lost his soul (Luke 22:21-23). The following is a list of the Bible's prohibitions against dabbling in the black arts:

Witchcraft (sorcery)—Exodus 22:18
Necromancy-Spiritualism—Leviticus 19:31; 20:6; Deuteronomy 18:11
Astrology—Isaiah 47:13
False prophecy
    inaccurate—Deuteronomy 18:20-22; cf. I John 4:1
    idolatrous—Deuteronomy 13:1-3
Divination—Deuteronomy 18:10
    arrows—Ezekiel 21:21
    livers—Ezekiel 21:21
    images—Ezekiel 21:21
Fire walking—Deuteronomy 18:10
Omens—Jeremiah 10:2
Wizardry (secret knowledge)—Deuteronomy 18:11
Charms (snakes)—Jeremiah 8:17

Enchantment (spells)—Isaiah 47:9-12

Times (lucky days)—Leviticus 19:26

The term translated "witch" by the King James Version is more accurately rendered "sorcerer."[22]

The Bible gives us the answers we need to live a full and abundant life. Messing with hidden things is messing with trouble. "The secret things belong to the LORD our God, but the things revealed belong to us and to our sons forever, that we may observe all the words of this law" (Deuteronomy 29:29).

To put yourself under the authority, and thus, the power, of another being is an act of rebellion against God. It will lead to disastrous results. But worst of all, submission to the occult is a way of despising God; it is disobedience of the highest order. "For rebellion is as the sin of divination, and insubordination is as iniquity and idolatry" (1 Samuel 15:23). It is no accident that divination and immorality are so often mentioned in the same context (Acts 15:29; 1 Corinthians 10:6-9; Galatians 5:20; Revelation 2:14; 9:21). Those who choose the occult over Christ want power and authority apart from Him. This is the worldview of the Satanist as expressed by Anton Szandor La Vey, who founded the San Francisco-based Church of Satan in 1969: "I wouldn't presume to improve on Milton's quote, 'Better to reign in hell than serve in heaven.'"[23]

FLIM-FLAM

One last point needs to be made. While there are probably occult phenomena that are truly linked to the demonic, most of what is passed off as "supernatural" is nothing more than flim-flam. Some people are ready to believe almost anything. Even in an era in which science is still king, a good many suckers are still born. Some of the most rational people become unbelievably irrational when it comes to psychic phenomena. You might get sucked into groups that promote themselves through flim-flam, believing that they "have the power." Flim-flam is the art of the con. As George C. Scott said in the movie *The Flim-Flam Man*, "You can't cheat an honest man." When it comes to psychic phenomena, you can't fool a rational man who understands the limits of the devil, the ingenuity of fakers, and the gullibility of the naive.

All of us want to believe in supernatural powers. This one fact is used by some very talented but evil people to draw spiritual seekers into dangerous spiritual movements. The vulnerable and desperate are the most susceptible. You may be shown what seems to be supernatural phenomena to attract you to a particular cult, pseudo-Christian religious group, or the occult. If you are particularly depressed, confused, or just desperate for answers, you might find yourself attracted to some of the most bizarre and sinister religious movements. Don't say "It can't happen to me." It happened to nine hundred desperate souls in Guyana, South America:

> "Reverend" Jim Jones was as charismatic a leader as any who ever swayed reason. Despite his farcical philosophy, he managed to convince a considerable number of California's populace that he had a direct pipeline to the gods and to salvation. With the kind of sleight of hand and sleight of mind that characterizes such charlatans, he "proved" that he could raise the dead—he performed the "miracle" forty-seven times in his church—and showed his followers that he was able to cure cancer and other afflictions by removing masses of organic junk from their bodies. After his death, cult members came forward to testify that, after threats from Jones, they had agreed to fake death and then stage instant resurrections. The surgery was even simpler than that still being performed by "psychic surgeons" of Brazil and the Philippines. Jones merely reached beneath the clothes of the intimidated faithful and pulled out chicken gizzards and other material, according to witnesses. Those who did not see through the tricks were convinced.[24]

Jones had his followers believing that he had supernatural powers. They would do anything for such a man. Over nine hundred of them followed him in death. Most of them went willingly.

Danny Korem, a world-famous magician, writes that it is possible "to convince almost anybody—under the right circumstances and through the use of trickery—that one may have supernatural powers." Korem argues "that unless one is schooled in how the mind can be deceived, one is at a potential disadvantage when trying to objectively report so-called manifestations of occult powers."[25]

Most of you probably know of Sherlock Holmes, the fictionalized English master detective. Holmes's creator was Sir Arthur Conan Doyle. Holmes the character is quite different from Doyle the author. As a detective, Holmes was scrupulously rational. He could deduce the most fantastic clues from only a few scraps of evidence. The angle of a stab wound would tell him the height of the assailant. A whiff of tobacco

THE OCCULT EXPLOSION

smoke left lingering at the scene of a crime would enable him to trace the thief through a local tobacco shop that blended the odd mixture. Everything was logical and reasonable. There had to be a rational explanation for even the most suspicious circumstances, even those in which the clues seemed to point to the paranormal. For Holmes, there was always a rational explanation.

But when it came to psychic phenomena, Sir Arthur Conan Doyle became especially irrational. On this issue, he did not personify Sherlock Holmes. He was willing to believe any fragment of evidence to support his unbending belief that mediums could penetrate the realm of the supernatural and communicate with departed spirits. Then he met up with Harry Houdini, the "Handcuff King."

Harry Houdini was the most famous magician who ever lived. His name is synonymous with magic. He could escape from any and all restraining devices: handcuffs, straight jackets, safes, locked boxes, and jails. He once escaped from Scotland Yard. He even escaped after being placed *inside* a locked safe.

Houdini was fascinated with life beyond the senses. He had a running battle with Sir Arthur Conan Doyle about the legitimacy of contacting the spirit world. Sir Arthur believed that certain people had the "gift" of being able to break through to the other side. Houdini wanted so much to believe, but could not. "I'm not denouncing spiritualism. I'm showing up frauds. If there is an honest medium, trot her out."[26]

Doyle was convinced that Houdini was himself a medium, capable of supernatural feats. He believed that Houdini could perform some of his tricks only by dematerializing himself and rematerializing himself later. Houdini objected.

> I do claim to free myself from the restraint of fetters and confinement, but positively state that I accomplish my purpose purely by physical, not psychical means. The force necessary to "shoot a bolt within a lock," is drawn from Houdini the living human being and not a medium. My methods are perfectly natural, resting on natural laws of physics. I do not *dematerialize* or *materialize* anything; I simply control and manipulate natural things in a manner perfectly well known to myself, and thoroughly accountable for and adequately understandable (if not duplicable) by any person to whom I may elect to divulge my secrets.[27]

In one sense Houdini should be an example to us all. Don't be afraid to question the supposed-supernatural, especially when it's linked to the occult. If you are ever tempted to believe, then investigate, question, and doubt. Don't be afraid to "test the spirits." This can also mean calling on an expert to help you out. On the other hand, we should never forget that occult phenomena can be real, although I suspect that the many reported occurrences are nothing more than wishful thinking, fakery, deception, and flim-flam. Again, if you believe it to be real, flee from evil.

> "See to it that no one takes you captive through philosophy and empty deception, according to the tradition of men, according to the elementary principles of the world, rather than according to Christ" (Colossians 2:8).

CONCLUSION

With the erosion and decline of a Christian culture, we have seen the vacuum filled by a revival of beliefs that would have been unthinkable when a vibrant Christian culture flourished. The occult is the last spiral down into the void. It's man's last desperate lunge for answers. If this is the best the non-Christian worldview can offer, then we can expect a resurgence of the Christian worldview. There is no hope in a worldview that can only offer sorrow and tragedy. But if we are to keep the "encircling eyes" at bay, we must once again build high the fire of a comprehensive Christian worldview.

An ax sticking out of a victim's head is standard fare in Hollywood, and it is becoming standard fare for television. On a television episode of *Friday the 13th: The Series*, a satanically possessed villain opened his mouth, inserted the twin barrels of a shotgun and pulled the trigger. Horror, macabre, and the occult are now stirred together to make a bizarre witch's brew. Occult and horror themes are standard viewing options in our day when anything and everything goes.

> Several years ago, when television producer Aaron Spelling tried to persuade Stephen King to write a TV horror show, the author of "Salem's Lot," "Carrie," and "The Shining" said he would do it on one condition.

> I've always remembered an episode of Boris Karloff's "Thriller" where the hero's murdered brother came walking downstairs with an ax sticking out of his head," King recalls. "It scared the daylights out of me."

THE OCCULT EXPLOSION

"I told Spelling, 'Boy, if we could get away with anything like that on network TV, you've got yourself a deal.' Spelling told me, 'Well, maybe we could have the ax sticking out of his shoulder,' and I said, 'No, no, sorry.'"[28]

There was a time when occult themes were handled in semi-biblical fashion at the movies and on television. Evil was real, there was a personal God who governed the universe, and the devil always got what was coming to him. But if you watch contemporary movies dealing with horror, the occult, and the demonic, you will find that evil often has the upper hand. It's endless sequels of *Nightmare on Elm Street*. Freddy Kruger even made it to the television screen in *Nightmare on Elm Street: Freddy's Nightmares*. You just can't keep the devil down for very long, especially in Hollywood. And if this is not enough, we have to endure countless sequels of the *Halloween* saga. And Jason is always back in *Friday the 13th*.

While they might frighten a viewer or two, very few people believe that the story lines express anything about the real world. The return of Michael in *Halloween* is little different from Dr. Frankenstein's original monster returning in the *Bride of Frankenstein*. As we learn in the sequel *Bride*, the monster, played by Boris Karloff, had not really died as the floor of the windmill collapsed and he plummeted to the cellar. And Dr. Frankenstein somehow survived being thrown from the windmill. Of course, the sequel would never had been made if the initial *Frankenstein* movie had bombed at the box office.

Movie-goers will put up with being frightened by things they know aren't real. Viewers can move from the created world of fantasy—and even horror—and immediately return to reality once the credits roll and the lights are turned on. No harm is initially done. But through this process, evil is trivialized.

The secularist does not know how to deal with the topic of the demonic. He will either dismiss the devil as a relic of a superstitious age, or embrace the demonic worldview as a viable option. In our progressively anti-Christian culture, the devil will more often be dismissed than embraced. In either case, the devil wins. Christians must remember, however, that his victory is brief and his doom is sure.

8
LIVING IN A POSTMODERN WORLD

> Under the post-modern onslaught, all boundaries and distinctions rapidly fall. Some of the losses associated with the collapse of traditional distinctions have been trivial, but others have been earthshaking, and there seems to be no way to distinguish between the two in the post-modern context. People no longer know where the lines fall.[1]

"BEAUTY is in the eye of the beholder." Many of us have uttered these words at some point in time. But few of us have really thought about the implications of this little phrase. Its message is that objective standards for beauty do not exist and that virtue is arbitrarily defined by individuals. What may be beautiful to you may not be beautiful to someone else, and what one perceives as ugly may be truly exquisite to another.

Perhaps this criticism simply nit-picks an innocent phrase that has seen many adolescents through the more insecure years of life. However, the *implication* of this phrase—the supremacy of subjectivity and relativism—is becoming the worldview of many Americans today. Modern society generally believes that *truth*, as well as beauty, is in the eye of the beholder. Truth is not objective, something that exists apart from us; rather, truth is "what works for us." This emerging perspective denies *standards* and argues that truth is relative to individuals or cultures.

The greatest offense to the unbeliever is the Christian's insistence that there is only one truth. The statement that Jesus is the *only* way, the *only* truth, and the *only* light seems rather closed-minded. For secularists, it seems reasonable that if there is a "God," people should be able to worship him (or her or it) however they choose. In fact, George Barna of the

Barna Research Group found that 62% of all Americans believe that all religious faiths teach the same lessons about life. Barna also found that while 60% of all Americans believe that the Bible is totally accurate in all of its teachings, 70% believe that there are no absolutes! This general lack of foundation is reflected in the title of Barna's current book on what people believe, *Absolute Confusion*.[2] Indeed, confusion is the spirit of the age.

A new worldview is emerging, a worldview that calls into question all traditional notions of truth, structure, and reality. It is called *postmodernism*. Postmodernism removes the anchor of objective truth and pushes human experience into the chaotic sea of human preference and subjectivity. Postmodernism says that while absolute truth was once a viable belief, it has turned out to be little more than a passing fad.

What is the source of this absurdity? For many of us the notion that there is no objective truth is foolish, and yet this idea is becoming increasingly entrenched in our society. Who would question the scientific truth that light travels at 186,282 miles per second, or that the law of non-contradiction is a fundamental rule of logic? Better yet, who would question that $2 + 2 = 4$, or that Jesus is the only way to the Father? Answer: people who seek more consistency in their rejection of God. Fact and certainty are not acceptable to people who deny universal standards. What we are seeing today is a worldview shift, from the modern to the postmodern.[3]

BACKGROUND

Shifts in worldview are nothing new. Western thought has undergone continual change. As Gene Veith puts it, "One worldview follows another. In the eighteenth century the Enlightenment challenged the Biblical synthesis that had dominated Western culture. With the nineteenth century came both romanticism and scientific materialism. The twentieth century has given us Marxism and fascism, positivism and existentialism."[4] But before we can discuss postmodernism, we need to first take a look at the periods that preceded it: the *premodern* and the *modern*.

The Premodern Age

The premodern age, as it is condescendingly called, is the period in intellectual history that encompasses all thought from ancient Greek philosophy, through the Renaissance and the Reformation, up until the dawn of the Enlightenment. Of course, not every one agrees with when the premodern era concluded and the modern era commenced. A great deal of overlap is present in any worldview transition.

Premodernism, like modernism after it, was a multi-faceted phase of Western culture that cannot be characterized by any one worldview. As Veith puts it, it was a "complex, dynamic, tension-filled era [which] included mythological paganism and classical rationalism, as well as Biblical revelation."[5] But for all of its diversity, the period is marked by a strong belief in the supernatural and in absolute truth.

For example, Plato believed that the natural world manifested so much diversity and change that a supernatural world must exist to establish coherence and meaning. During the Medieval period, the Christian worldview came to dominate this pursuit of the supernatural. This worldview stated that God is the foundation of truth and the purpose of man is to discern his relationship to God. Throughout this premodern period, great Christian theologians flourished, men such as Augustine, Thomas Aquinas, Blaise Pascal, Martin Luther, and John Calvin. Belief in absolute truth and the supernatural was non-negotiable. Premoderns acknowledged that God's unifying truth was the basis for understanding reality as a *universe*, not a *multiverse*.[6]

The Modern Age

The fallen nature of humanity, inclining towards autonomy, made a shift in worldviews inevitable. Man no longer needed to be bound by the superstitious, out-dated beliefs of the past. Modern man did not need the supernatural to guide him; reason and science alone could give him the answers he needed to understand the universe. This paradigm shift from premodern to modern was realized in the period historians have referred to as the Enlightenment.

For many, the Enlightenment was the birth of the "modern" period in intellectual history. Some historians date this period as beginning with the French Revolution in 1789, and ending with the fall of the Berlin Wall in 1989.[7] While many Enlightenment thinkers did not completely reject belief in God, they banished Him to the remotest corner of the heavens. If God did exist, He was neither concerned nor involved in His creation. Reason and science were now the objects of worship, and redemption for mankind was to be found in their study and application.

Others believe that the modern age commenced even earlier, with the Copernican revolution. Both Aristotle (384-322 B.C.) and Claudius Ptolemaeus (90?-168? A.D.), widely known as Ptolemy, had maintained that the earth was the physical center of the universe. Even the church adopted their views. The Polish astronomer Nicolaus Copernicus (1473-1543) questioned their cosmology and the church's support of it. In the case of Copernicus, and later Galileo (1564-1642) and Johannes Kepler (1571-1630), mathematics was the governing principle to understand the movements of the planets around the sun.

While Copernicus, Kepler, and Galileo all believed in God, they inadvertently set in motion a purely mechanical understanding of the working of the universe. Their emphasis on mathematical applications, as well as Isaac Newton's geometric interpretation of the universe, allowed modernists to embrace a purely mechanistic explanation for all of life. "Science inclined increasingly toward God the Watchmaker," and in time "suggested that God did not have to wind His watch after all—the universe more and more seemed given over by its Maker to impersonal natural laws."[8] The idea that the mechanistic world is governed by impersonal natural laws with no need of divine operation affected thought beyond the mathematical and theoretical.

> The transformation appeared everywhere. Montesquieu explained the development of institutions and national character as resulting from climate. Adam Smith expounded laws of political economy governing the wealth of nations. Gibbon, disinclined to sweeping general laws, nevertheless refined a historiography of purely natural causes, from which all trace of divine purpose vanished. Voltaire speculated on the social origins of morality. The greatest audacity was reserved for David Hume, whose "Natural History of Religion" calmly put religious belief on a par with other natural phenomena and traced its genesis to human efforts to quell fear of the unknown and allay anxieties over the uncertainties of life.[9]

For scientists and social theorists, God was not denied; He was simply redefined. Where He once providentially guided His creation and creatures, "He now appeared to have left the running of the world to impersonal laws."[10]

Now that God had been given the role of the Divine Engineer who was removed from any meaningful contact with the universe, a new paradigm was needed to make sense of the world. Modern worldviews such as *positivism* sought to unify the sciences and order human life by finding the basic pattern to explain human nature.[11] *Secular Humanism* emphasized the autonomy of the individual and the primacy of the intellect. Man could solve the problems of society through his own efforts, especially through education and technology.[12] Modernism taught that certain knowledge of ourselves and the world was possible because nature was a closed, static system of natural laws waiting to be discovered. Modernism did not deny certainty or fact, but made man his own god, to determine those truths for himself.

Unlike premodernism before it, modernism rejected the supernatural and proclaimed the sufficiency of logic and normal sense experience. Even biblical scholarship was tainted by this high evaluation of man; reliance upon *reason* instead of *revelation* became the basis for so-called higher criticism.[13] These higher critics rejected miracles, the incarnation, and other supernatural doctrines. Modernist scholars sought to "demythologize" the Bible and free it from the superstitious shackles that had bound it for so long. As Diogenes Allen observes:

> In time some went so far as to claim that the Bible was not needed at all. It was useful to the human race in its infancy, but now that we have achieved enlightenment, we can read the book of nature and avoid all the blemishes, distortions, and absurdities that are found in the Bible.[14]

Eventually this new "naturalistic" religion removed God from the picture altogether and attempted to produce a just and egalitarian social order that would embody reason and social progress.[15]

As it turned out, modernism did not produce the harmony that its prophets predicted. After slavery, two world wars, communism, Nazism, and nuclear bombs, people began to wonder whether the modern mind was really the road to paradise. They questioned modernism's confidence in reason, technology and science. In addition, the belief that nature is inherently orderly and governed by fixed, natural laws came under strong scrutiny. Scholars began to question the idea of absolutes in science[16] and logic[17] and became convinced that nature seems to be inherently disorderly and illusive.[18]

> Postmodernism grew out of disillusionment with modernism's failure to produce a perfect, rational, planned, and compassionate world. The dreams of modernity were admirable but in the light of contemporary history seem naive. Loss of faith in society's perfectibility through centralized planning and technological development arose in Europe and the United States throughout

the mid-twentieth century, and by 1990, with the collapse of centralized communism in the Soviet Union and Eastern Europe and the push toward deregulation and privatization in the United States and Great Britain, modernism was no longer a central force in economic planning or political thinking.[19]

In addition to admitting a chaotic universe, modern scholars began to criticize the idea that man is simply an unbiased observer of nature: "The mind is not the passive reflector of an external world and intrinsic order, *but is active and creative* in the process of perception and cognition. Reality is in some sense constructed by the mind, not simply perceived by it, and many such constructions are possible, *none necessarily sovereign*."[20]

Modernism's idea that man is simply a uniform product of nature was dying fast. By reducing the human condition to logic and scientific method, modernism denied the human *spirit*. Man was simply the result of a random assimilation of atoms, subject to the laws of nature in a closed universe. Freedom was an illusion, and determinism was reality. In fact, modernism could not account for the complexity of man's immaterial tendencies other than by appealing to bio-chemical reactions.[21] Darwinism, itself the child of modernism, has turned on its parent and killed modernism. As legal scholar Phillip Johnson observes:

> Modernism is the condition that begins when humans understand that God is really dead and that they therefore have to decide all the big questions for themselves. Modernism at times produces an exhilarating sense of liberation: we can do whatever we like, because there is no unimpeachable authority to prevent us. Modernism at other times is downright scary: how can we persuade other people that what *they* want to do to us is barred by some unchallengeable moral absolute?[22]

Modernism had delivered the very opposite of what it had promised. Its promises of liberation turned out to be masks for oppression and domination. By removing God and enthroning reason and science, man was now free to do all of the unrestrained evil he was capable of—all in the name of scientific progress. He soon discovered, however, that his self-made liberation had become his prison. Modernism, like pre-modernism before it, was now vulnerable. Reason and technology were really not messiahs, and the human spirit was still striving for its freedom and autonomy. Disillusioned by modernism, secular scholars were ready to consider a new system.

LIVING IN A POSTMODERN WORLD

THE SLIDE TO POSTMODERNISM

Shifts in worldviews take time even though single events seem to mark their transition period. Seemingly unrelated events and thoughts work their wizardry to produce unfathomable results. Once the shift has taken place, only a retrospective look will reveal the philosophical ebbs and flows that erode worldview landscapes. The twentieth century began on an optimistic note but quickly lost its idealism as war engulfed the world. World War I "shattered much of Europe's already fading optimism, and the advent of Nazis and fascists shook men's confidence in their present and their past."[23]

Despite world war, belief in evolutionary progress had not lost its luster. In 1920, the English novelist H. G. Wells wrote *The Outline of History*, described as "a song of evolutionary idealism, faith in progress, and complete optimism."[24] before too long, Wells began to lose hope in what he believed would be the inevitabilities of evolutionary advancement and social enrichment. "By 1933, when he published *The Shape of Things to Come*, he could see no better way to overcome the stubbornness and selfishness between people and nations than a desperate action by intellectual idealists to seize control of the world by force and establish their vision with a universal compulsory educational program."[25] An elite class of social engineers would be needed to force the "good society" on people whether they wanted it or not. "Finally, shortly before his death, [Wells] wrote an aptly-titled book, *The Mind at the End of Its Tether* (1945) in which he concluded that 'there is no way out, or around, or through the impasse. It is the end.'"[26]

The outlook in America was different. A form of secular optimism prevailed after World War II that even a police action in Korea in the 1950s could not dampen. America had never known defeat in war, and her countryside had not been ravaged by incendiary bombs or nuclear fallout. She was on a roll.

The post-war optimism continued with the inauguration of President John F. Kennedy in 1960 and dreams of "Camelot."[27] Modernism was running full throttle in the early '60s with its great scientific advances—man was about to conquer the heavens and put a man on the moon—and official judicial statements of atheism with prayer and Bible reading removed from America's public schools. The theistic house cleaning was now nearly complete. Since 1859, the year that Darwin's *Origin of Species* was published, modern man had been trying to rid the universe of God and the supernatural. America was about to show the world what man could do without God.

On November 22, 1963, gunfire put an end to the euphoria. As one child of the '60s put it, "When Kennedy was killed is when America changed."[28] As if overnight, everything seemed to change. "Tennessee-born photographer Jim Smith, who describes his experience of the Sixties as 'having my world view torn apart with nothing to replace it,' says that 'the Kennedy assassination really was the trigger.'"[29] The following social chaos was hardly encouraging to an idealistic generation:

> Lyndon Johnson's skillfully and ruthlessly imposed legislative substance—the final culmination of the old Progressive optimism—soon turned to dust in the mouths of his followers. The Vietnam war, race riots, and the deficit-induced price inflation broke the spirit of the age. Johnson could not be re-elected in 1968, just four years after he was elected President.[30]

From visions of Camelot to chants of "Hey! Hey! LBJ! How many kids didja kill today?" America was abandoning what little faith it had in the secular faith of modernism. As if tens of thousands of dead young men were not enough to destroy the worldview of modernism the murder of two cultural icons confirmed the disintegration of society. "With the assassinations of King and Robert Kennedy, we lost our last hope of combating racism or ending the war through the System, and the System lost our consent."[31]

A crisis of secular faith had emerged. The new generation questioned the orthodoxy of rational neutrality. The guardians of modernism had sent young men and women to the rice paddies of Vietnam, and more than 58,000 of them had returned in coffins, 153,000 returned severely wounded, and an equal amount more lightly wounded. A break with the past was unavoidable. People were calling for "revolution." They "wanted apocalypse, Utopia,"[32] a world transformed. Transformed by what? That was the question. Drugs, sexual experimentation, Eastern philosophy, and the occult were all viable options. The counter culture of the '60s wanted something more than the impersonalism offered by rationalism. In fact, the best and the brightest of the rationalists had sent America's youth to Southeast Asia to die.[33] For the first time in her history, America had lost a war.

Postmodernism is the logical outworking of modernism. Stephen Connor says that the "concept of postmodernism cannot be said to have crystallized until about the mid-1970's. . . ."[34] Modernism had received some strong criticism, and it was becoming more and more tenable to

LIVING IN A POSTMODERN WORLD

assert that the postmodern had come to stay, but it took some time before scholarship really jumped on the bandwagon.[35] Events, violent events, forced the hands of the academic community.

> If May 4, 1970, was the day that the war between the generations and classes of white America became a war in earnest, in retrospect it was also the day that war began to end. It was as if the rising tensions had needed to climax in the taking of life. After the strikes in the wake of Kent, the energy of confrontation began to ebb.[36]

But little was resolved. The four protestors who were killed at Kent State University, through no will of their own, put an end to a misguided revolution. The worldview of modernism was buried with them. The campuses in the '70s, and even through the '80s, remained eerily quiet. The silence, however, was not a sign of inaction. A new worldview was being developed without fanfare—a quiet revolution.

DEFINING POSTMODERNISM

What is postmodernism? The system is both complex and ambiguous, but, basically speaking, postmodernism is anti-worldview.[37] It denies the existence of any universal truth and questions every worldview. The postmodernist will not tolerate any worldview that claims to be universal in application. But this is not enough. The goal of postmodernism is not only to reject worldviews as oppressive, but also to reject even the possibility of *having* a coherent worldview.

There are many worldviews around today, and the postmodernist believes that it is his responsibility to critique each one. Worldviews must be "flattened out," so that no one particular approach or belief is more "true" than any other. What constitutes truth, then, is relative to the individual or community holding the belief.

Whereas modernism and Christianity clashed by each claiming truth, postmodernism attacks the concept of truth itself. For postmodernism, truth is simply "what works for you." Postmodernism, then, claims to be not so much an *orthodoxy* (a positive belief system or worldview), as an *orthopraxy* (a series of methods for analysis).

In the postmodern world man does not sit back and passively receive knowledge about the world; rather, man's interpretation *is* reality. This confusion of subject and object has correctly labeled postmodernism as nihilistic and relativistic.[38] Nothing is absolute; logic, science, history, and morality are merely the products of individual experience and interpretation.

The postmodernist will declare that reality is only what we perceive it to be. By adopting such a view, however, he now has a problem. As such, reality is unknowable. Charles Mackenzie observes: "If in knowing an object the human mind virtually creates knowledge, the question has been raised then, What is the external world when it is not being perceived?"[39] For the postmodernist, the only thing that can be known is personal experience and interpretations of that experience. Man can know nothing in any absolute sense. All one has is his own finite, limited experience. Logic, science, history, and ethics are human disciplines that must, and do, reflect human insufficiency and subjectivity.

In issues of morality no one particular view is foundational. Rather, each culture's, and ultimately each individual's, view of ethics is just as valid as the next. This view is the basis for "multiculturalism" and the "political correctness" movement in today's society. Rather than affirming any one morality as absolute, every person's moral persuasion must be respected no matter what it is, and language must be revised so as to erase all offensive and narrow-minded perspectives.

ASSESSING THE POSTMODERN WORLDVIEW

Postmodernism correctly questions modernism's reliance upon logic and science as certain paths to truth. The fact that philosophies of logic, science, and ethics are constantly changing shows that man without God cannot attain uniformity or ultimate standards. Modernism's unswerving faith in man was a foolish extreme. But postmodernism, even with its rejection of modernism's claims, pushes another extreme. Postmodernism's rejection of "absolute truth" undermines its own position. On what basis ought the postmodernist view be taken as *true*? Is its denial of "absolute truth" itself absolute? In other words, how can the postmodernist claim that his way of looking at things is "true" all the while denying the concept of truth?

The fact is that even as postmodernism denies all worldviews, it is itself a worldview. It is not just a system of analysis, because it must have a view on reality, knowledge, and morality in order to discern and justify its methods. Postmodernism is riddled with assumptions, in need of as much scrutiny and evaluation as any other worldview. The postmodernist must absolutize his claims to get his system going. This kind of extreme relativism is impossible; it affirms what it denies. Likewise, if language is all there is to reality, and all interpretation is subjective, then why do postmodernists write books? Why believe that there is any possible way to *communicate*? How do we in fact know that the reader's interpretation was the author's intent? This view of language, then, becomes the prison house of postmodern thought.

On a societal note, while postmodernism tries to enhance understanding of the diversity among people, it actually creates a new tribalism. Multiculturalism says that the traditional idea of America, as an assimilation of cultures, is false. America is not a "melting pot," but rather more like a "salad bowl." So everything—education, morality, politics, etc.—is defined by cultural interests. History, for example, is no longer an acquisition of knowledge of past events; rather, it is revised so as to enhance the self-image of a particular group that has been excluded or "oppressed." As Veith observes:

> Contemporary scholars seek to dismantle the paradigms of the past and "to bring the marginal into the center" (rewriting history in favor of those who have been excluded from power—women, homosexuals, blacks, Native Americans, and other victims of oppression). Scholars attack received ideas with withering skepticism, while constructing new models as alternatives. Those who celebrate the achievements of Western civilization are accused of narrow-minded "Euro-centrism"; this view is challenged by "Afro-centrism," which exalts Africa as the pinnacle of civilization. Male-dominant thought is replaced by feminist models. "Patriarchal religions" such as Judaism and Christianity are challenged and replaced with matriarchal religions; the influence of the Bible is countered by the influence of "goddess-worship." Homosexuality is no longer considered a psychological problem; rather, homophobia is.[40]

It does not matter what *actually* happened in the worldview shift from modernism to postmodernism; that is impossible to know and as such is irrelevant. It is crucial, however, that we recognize the anti-Christian and self-contradictory message of postmodernism: all beliefs must be tolerated except for the belief that denies that all beliefs must be tolerated. In essence, postmodernism is at war with the Christian worldview. Power is its goal—power for man apart from God. Remember, postmodernism rejects the idea of any universal truth, whether it is history, logic, or Christ.

IS POSTMODERNISM ALL BAD?

Irving Kristol, a fellow at the American Enterprise Institute, describes the current time as "a shaking of the foundations of the modern world."[41] Other scholars agree:

> A massive intellectual revolution is taking place that is perhaps as great as that which marked off the modern world from the Middle Ages. . . . The principles forged during the Enlightenment . . . which formed the foundations of the modern mentality, are crumbling.[42]

The collapse of Enlightenment humanism is imminent; it is being attacked from all angles. From religious conservatives to scientific liberals, the shared goal is to overhaul the presuppositions of modernism, although their motives differ greatly. Christians welcome the opportunity for credible public discourse, and many scientists are eager to see a shift in scientific outlook that will account for the anomalies that modern science has avoided. These are exciting times, times in which the church should be alert.

The all-sufficiency of human reason and science is now under fire, and the supernatural—that which is not empirical—is once again open to consideration. The marketplace of ideas is wide open. The church must understand the nature of our age and how Christians can respond to a world increasingly steeped in dissolution. In a postmodern world Christianity is intellectually relevant.[43]

Not only has postmodernism opened the cultural door once again to the Christian faith, but with its critical apparatus it also offers a few lessons for the church to learn. Veith likens the current situation to that of the pagans at the Tower of Babel.[44] Genesis 11:1-9 tells us that at one time everyone in the whole earth spoke the same language. As some were traveling east, they stopped in the valley of Shinar to make a name for themselves by building a tower that would reach into heaven. When the Lord saw what they were doing, He came down and destroyed the heart of their unity: language. As a result, they were scattered over the earth without a way to communicate.

Modern man also built his tower of autonomy. He removed God (so he thought) and placed himself on the throne of his world. But postmodernism demanded that this man-based philosophy be taken to its logical extension of nihilism. It is interesting that postmodernism strikes at the

LIVING IN A POSTMODERN WORLD

very same thing God did: language. Outside absolute standards, language is reduced to pure subjectivity. And, without language, logic and science are meaningless; they have no application. As we have seen, postmodernism isolates each man in his own private world. The arrogant, pseudo-unity that man had claimed to find was now just a foolish dream. Like the people at the Tower of Babel, modern man has been fragmented and scattered. There is no center of discourse any longer.

In this light, perhaps the most significant contribution of postmodernism is that it reminds us of our finitude. It reminds us that without God mankind is relegated to absurdity. By default, it tells us that God must be the beginning of all of our thinking, that apart from Him we can know nothing. It is the fear of the Lord that is the *beginning* of knowledge (Proverbs 1:7), not the conclusion of our investigation. In Christ "are hidden all of the treasures of wisdom and knowledge" (Colossians 2:3). This does not mean that we reject disciplines such as logic and science. We see them as *tools* to better understand God's amazing creation, not as *ultimate standards* which take the place of God's revelation. After all, the "gift of logical reason was given by God to man in order that he might order the revelation of God for himself."[45] Science is simply the study of God's creation, so that we might better understand how to care for it, advance in knowledge, and fulfill the cultural mandate.[46]

In the same way, postmodernism reminds us that, like logic, theology is not exhaustive but a developing science. There are many approaches to theology, none exhaustive. It is the theologian's responsibility to examine carefully all propositions in accordance with God's Word, and press forward to better understand the revelation that God has given. We are to think God's thoughts after him.

For our personal lives, postmodernism shows us the futility of autonomy. It forces those of us who know Christ back to the basics of depending on Christ for everything—from salvation to social standards. Only in Christ does man have meaning and purpose; He is the vine, we are the branches, and apart from him we can do nothing (John 15:15).

In conclusion, postmodernism need not be seen as a mortal enemy. In many ways it drives us back to complete and total dependence on God. It reminds us that He is the foundation for every area of life, whether it be logic or law. It shows us that there are no neutral areas of life in which man reigns. Postmodernism points out that we all have presuppositions, and that no one is unbiased. We all bring our assumptions to our experience; each fact about the world is theory-laden. The question then becomes, Which presuppositions are true? The answer is clear: the Christian worldview is true. Christianity alone is the escape from subjective nihilism, for it alone provides the necessary foundations to make the facts intelligible.

Postmodernism has broken the stiff neck of humanistic modernism. As man seeks consistency in his anarchy, he will watch his futile autonomy trickle from his clutches into a pile of dust at his feet. It is the church's duty now to answer the world's wail of despair. Throughout all ages and into eternity, man's deepest yearnings will only be filled in Christ.

CONCLUSION

Archimedes (287-212 B.C.), the Greek mathematician and physicist who yelled *Eureka!*—"I have found it!"—as he ran naked from his bathtub at the discovery of the principle of displacement, once boasted that given the proper lever, and given a place to stand, he could "move the earth." But upon what would Archimedes stand to accomplish such a feat? Certainly not on the earth. Archimedes needed a place to stand *outside* the earth, a place *different* from the earth he wanted to move. His lever needed a fulcrum. This, too, had to rest on something.

Atlas of Greek mythology (son of a Titan and brother of Prometheus), had a similar problem. Atlas was condemned by Zeus to stand eternally at the western end of the earth to hold up the sky. In artistic renditions, however, Atlas is depicted as holding up the world. But what is Atlas using for his support of the earth? What is he standing upon?

All argumentation will inevitably require the arguer to establish the authority that gives credibility to his worldview. That reference point, for example, might be the expert opinion of others. Of course, these experts are not ultimate authorities. They also appeal to some decisive standard. "[J]ust because most of the authorities in a field are shouting in unison that they know the truth, it ain't necessarily so."[1] It is upon a final standard—a standard to which no greater appeal is made—that all worldviews rest.

> At the center of every world-view is what might be called the "touchstone proposition" of that world-view, a proposition that is held to be the fundamental truth about reality and serves as a criterion to determine which other propositions may or may not count as candidates for belief.[2]

The idea that a touchstone establishes authenticity, fineness, right and wrong, and justice is an old one. "In the days of the gold rush men used a touchstone, a fine grained dark stone, such as jasper, to determine the

WAR OF THE WORLDVIEWS

quality of the gold which they had discovered. Today a Geiger counter is used to locate uranium and other precious metals. In baseball the umpire makes the decisions in the contest between the pitcher and the batter. In the courtroom the judge decides questions of law. In their respective fields the touchstone, the Geiger counter, the umpire and the judge speak with authority."[3] So it is in the war over worldviews. Every worldview claims to be the touchstone. Each worldview claims that it defines for all competing worldviews what is true and right.

IDEAS HAVE CONSEQUENCES

In the eighteenth century Enlightenment philosophers confronted the presuppositions of the biblical worldview and adopted varieties of rationalism, empiricism, and mysticism to further their anti-Christian hostilities. The gauntlet was finally laid down with the publication of Darwin's *The Origin of Species*. Darwin's work was the weapon that the secularists needed to advance a rival comprehensive worldview based on non-theistic, that is, non-Christian, presuppositions. For the secularists Darwinian evolution was a way out of a world governed by a Creator.

German scholar Ernst Haeckel pushed the implications of Darwin's theories to comprehensive limits. He believed that moral law was subject to biology. "Thousands, indeed millions of cells are sacrificed in order for a species to survive."[4] He argued that if survival of the fittest is morally operative in biology, then it is equally ethical for society. "Haeckel's use of Darwin's theories was decisive in the intellectual history of his time. It united trends already developing in Germany of racism, imperialism, romanticism, nationalism, and anti-semitism."[5] In 1906, at the age of seventy-two, Haeckel founded the Monist League. To the Monist, man was *one* with nature and the animals. He was no special creation as the "image of God." He had no soul, only a superior degree of development. The Monist League "united eugenicists, biologists, theologians, literary figures, politicians and sociologists."[6]

The Darwinian worldview as expressed by Haeckel's Monist League was comprehensive in interpreting all of life in terms of evolution. The effects on Germany, as all of history attests, was disastrous. "Otto Ammon, a leading racial anthropologist, wrote that the laws of nature were the laws of society. 'Bravery, cunning and competition are virtues . . . Darwin[ism] must become the new religion of Germany . . . the racial struggle is necessary for mankind.'"[7]

Karl Marx also found in Darwin "the natural history foundation" for his views. Hegel's philosophy of "dialectical materialism," where con-

---
CONCLUSION
---

flicting views were synthesized into a third, more advanced stage of development, was now supported by Darwin's biology and inherent historical implications that "society, like nature, improved over time."[8]

Darwin had a similar impact on America, although not in the form of Nazism or Marxism. The American industrialist Andrew Carnegie embraced the social implications of Darwin's theories and applied them to the world of business. "That light came in as a flood and all was clear. Not only had I got rid of theology and the supernatural, but I found the truth of evolution."[9] John D. Rockefeller, using Darwinian logic, also believed that "The growth of a large business is merely the survival of the fittest."[10]

GOD MUST DIE

"What must be destroyed is the instrument used by the clergy to subjugate the masses, that is to say religion itself."[11] Religion, in this case the Christian religion, is the greatest threat to so-called "free thinkers" because it emphasizes that man is a *dependent* being. If there is a God, then man is obligated, in the words of the Christian astronomer and mathematician Johannes Kepler (1571-1630), to think God's thoughts after Him.[12] Such a hypothesis forces man to recognize that he is dependent upon God not only for knowledge (epistemology) but also for the way he lives (ethics). God must be eliminated if man is to ascend to the throne.

Anti-Christian sentiments have been voiced throughout this century. Christianity is the great enemy of those who place man at the center of the universe. "'The secular idea,' says an historian of secularism, 'includes a philosophical notion which rests upon the independence and capacity of reason.' When he embarked on his struggle against the Church, [Otto Von] Bismarck gave it a highly significant name: *Kulturkampf*, 'struggle for civilization,' pointing thereby to a collision between two concepts of civilization."[13]

ALL OF LIFE IS RELIGIOUS

It is often proposed that while Christians interpret reality from a religious perspective, non-Christians are neutral or non-religious in their evaluation of the facts. This is a myth. "Every human being has faith in something which affects his understanding of everything. . . . The premise that facts may be objectively known, absolutely uninfluenced by the faith of the knower, is simply untrue."[14] Religion is simply a belief in something as the greatest interpreting principle. Being religious does not necessarily mean believing in a personal god. Atheists are religious since they *believe* that god does not exist. Such a belief is a statement of faith.

The rejection of the God of Christianity brings with it the deification of man. Ernst Heinrich (1834-1919), a German biologist who popularized Darwinism in Central Europe, wrote: "The secret of theology is anthropology. God is man adoring himself. The Trinity is the human family deified."[15] The humanist philosophy of the nineteenth century trumpeted this: "Mankind, reign! This is your age—which is vainly denied by the voice of pious echoes." Ludwig Feuerbach (1804-1872), German philosopher and theologian, stated his exclusive man-centered worldview with the motto "*Homo homni deus*: 'Man is man's god.'"[16]

RENEWING THE MIND

The history of non-Christian philosophical thought offers ample evidence that fallen men and women need a trustworthy touchstone of truth. This necessity becomes even more obvious when we consider that the inevitable course or "development" of man-centered philosophical thought (or religious philosophy) moves from man's claim to knowledge on his own to skepticism and doubt regarding man's ability to know *anything* for certain. Such conflict occurred in ancient and medieval times and is reoccurring in our day. Only the acceptance of God's own revealed word (Scripture) can break this self-destructive philosophical cycle and allow man to know that he truly *can* know.

On the other hand, the Christian's authority, Scripture, prevents an individual from embracing irrationalism where thinking is abandoned in favor of mysticism. The mind certainly is the *vehicle* God uses to transmit His revelation to us, but the mind never is the *standard* by which we determine the reliability of that revelation.

Too often, however, Christians either believe without thinking or distort the thinking process by denying God as the reference point for right thinking. The Apostle Paul warns that even our zeal for God can be unfounded when true knowledge is ignored or suppressed: "For I bear them witness that they have a zeal for God, but not in accordance with knowledge" (Romans 10:2; 1:18-23). There are many who believe in "God," but it is a god of their own imagination (Romans 1:28).

Peter tells us to gird out minds for action (1 Peter 1:13). Scripture informs us that the mind is necessary to understand the will of God, but that, in its fallen nature, it is in a state of disrepair and in need of renewal

CONCLUSION

(Romans 12:2). Rousas J. Rushdoony rightly observes: "The Christian is not hostile to reason as reason, but to Reason as god. The Christian does not believe in reason; he believes in God and uses reason under God."[17] The unregenerate man is spiritually dead in "trespasses and sins" (Ephesians 2:1); the "god of this world has blinded the minds of the unbelieving" (2 Corinthians 4:4); the rebellious has his mind "set on the flesh" and therefore is "hostile toward God" (Romans 8:7); he does not understand (Romans 3:11), and in reality, "cannot understand" the things of God (1 Corinthians 2:14).

Of course, there is danger in depreciating the mind, and embracing a "mindless" Christianity. Some believe "because it is impossible" (attributed to Tertullian, c.160-240). One attribute that separates man from animals is man's ability to reason: "Do not be as the horse or as the mule which have no understanding, whose trappings include bit and bridle to hold them in check, otherwise they will not come near to you" (Psalm 32:9). The ethically rebellious are compared to non-rational animals: "When my heart was embittered, and I was pierced within, then I was senseless and ignorant; I was like a beast before Thee" (Psalm 73:21-22; cf. Daniel 4:28-33). The point is that the mind must be brought into proper focus; it is fallen but not eradicated. The mind is indispensable for thinking in a biblical way. God has revealed His redemptive message through words to our minds. We need ears to hear, eyes to see, and a mind to understand.

But some will say, "But I have 'the mind of Christ' (1 Corinthians 2:16), so I do not need to concern myself with reason, logic, and straight thinking." Having "the mind of Christ" means to evaluate all of life from a biblical perspective. The "mind of Christ" is equated with "the Spirit of God" (2:11) as set forth in Scripture. The "mind of Christ," therefore, is identical with what is "written" (2:9). Paul quotes a passage from Isaiah 64:4 where he states that God has made known to us in *written form* "things which eye has not seen and ear has not heard, and which have not entered the heart of man" (v. 9).

Paul moves from telling the Corinthians that "we have the mind of Christ" to chastising them for not acting on that reality. This means that the "mind of Christ" is not a passive state that automatically kicks into gear when thought is needed. This is why Paul tells them—those who have the "mind of Christ"—that "I, brethren, could not speak to you as to spiritual men, but as to men of flesh, as to babes in Christ" (3:1). The Apostle is calling on the Corinthians to think straight *in terms of Scripture*.

Christians are instructed, therefore, to "renew" their minds (Romans 12:2) and to "walk no longer just as the Gentiles also walk, in the futility of their mind, being darkened in their understanding, excluded from the life of God, because of the ignorance that is in them, because of the hardness of their heart" (Ephesians 4:17-18). Renewal comes by "the washing of regeneration and renewing by the Holy Spirit" (Titus 3:5). the Holy Spirit regenerates and makes the heart and mind new. We were once dead in trespasses and sins, but now we are alive unto God (Ephesians 2:1).

The newness of life, however, does not make us independent thinkers. As Christians, we still are subject to the final authority of God's Word. Renewal of the mind never should be seen as a means of freeing Christians from reliance on God as our unswerving and certain standard of authority. The Apostle Paul, who was able to debate the philosophers of his day (Acts 17), warned us about the deceitfulness of reasoning independently of God: "See to it that no one take you captive through philosophy and empty deception, according to the tradition of men, according to the elementary principles of the world, rather than according to Christ" (Colossians 2:8). For the Christian, therefore, "human reason is neither an autonomous master nor a useless appendage, but a servant of the resurrected Christ in the work of the extension of his Kingdom. According to the biblical story human reason, like man himself, is the good creation through the work of Christ and the Holy Spirit."[18]

God calls us to "reason together" (Isaiah 1:18), not as equal partners but as independent and all-knowing Creator and dependant and ignorant creatures. Therefore, let us offer up our hearts, souls, and *minds* to the service our Savior and King for the defense of the Christian worldview.

END NOTES

Preface

1. An account of this famous radio event can be found in Charles Higham, *Orson Welles: The Rise and Fall of an American Genius* (New York: St. Martin's Press, 1985), pp. 123-28. These extraterrestrial villains had made their debut in H. G. Wells's classic novel *The War of the Worlds*. A movie version came to the screen in 1958.
2. Scott Siegel and Barbara Siegel, *The Encyclopedia of Hollywood: An A-to-Z of the Heroes, Heroines, and History of American Film* (New York: Facts on File, 1990), p. 453.
3. Higham, *Orson Welles*, p. 128.
4. James Davison Hunter, *Culture Wars: The Struggle to Define America* (New York: Basic Books, 1991), p. 64.
5. For a discussion of citizenship, see Gary DeMar, *"You've Heard It Said": 15 Biblical Misconceptions that Render Christians Powerless* (Atlanta, GA: American Vision, 1991), pp. 117-30.
6. Charles C. Ryrie, *The Living End* (Old Tappan, NJ: Revell, 1976), p. 21.
7. Hal Lindsey, *The Late Great Planet Earth* (Grand Rapids, MI: Zondervan, 1970), p. 145.
8. Hal Lindsey, "The Great Cosmic Countdown," *Eternity* (January 1977), p. 21. Consider what happens to fish if the bowl is not cleaned. They die!
9. Ted Peters, *Futures: Human and Divine* (Atlanta, GA: John Knox, 1978), pp. 28, 29.
10. For further discussion of this topic, see DeMar, *"You've Heard It Said,"* pp. 136, 166-68, 170.
11. A. A. Hodge, *Evangelical Theology: Lectures on Doctrine* (Carlisle, PA: The Banner of Truth Trust, [1890] 1990), p. 283.
12. *Idem.*
13. A. A. Hodge, *Outlines of Theology* (New York: A. C. Armstrong and Son, 1891), pp. 283-84.

Introduction

1. Francis A. Schaeffer, *How Should We Then Live?*, in *The Complete Works of Francis A. Schaeffer*, 5 vols. (Westchester, IL: Crossway Books, 1982), vol. 5, p. 148.
2. Cotton Mather, *The Great Works of Christ in America*, 2 vols. (Edinburgh: The Banner of Truth Trust, [1702] 1979), vol. 1, p. 26.

Chapter 1 – Preparing for Battle

1. From the comic strip "Funky Winkerbean" by Tom Batiuk, Field Enterprises, 1980.
2. Cornelius Van Til, *Apologetics* (Phillipsburg, NJ: Presbyterian and Reformed, 1976), p. 1.
3. Greg L. Bahnsen, "The Reformation of Christian Apologetics," *Foundations of Christian Scholarship*, Gary North, ed. (Vallecito, CA: Ross House Books, 1976), pp. 194-95.
4. *Ibid.*, p. 198.
5. "The *Council of the Areopagus* was a venerable commission of the ex-magistrates which took its name from the hill where it originally convened. In popular parlance its title was shortened to the 'the Areopagus,' and in the first century it had transferred its location to the Stoa Basileios (or 'Royal Portico') in the city marketplace – where the Platonic dialogues tell us that Euthyphro went to try his father for impiety and where Socrates had been tried for corrupting the youth with foreign deities. Apparently the Council convened on Mar's hill in Paul's day only for trying cases of homicide. That Paul 'stood in the midst of the Areopagus' (v. 22) and 'went out from their midst' (v. 33) is much easier understood in terms of his appearance before the Council than his standing on the hill (cf. Acts 4:7).... [The commission] exercised jurisdiction over matters of religion and morals." Greg L. Bahnsen, "The Encounter of Jerusalem with Athens" in *Ashland Theological Bulletin*, Ashland Theological Seminary, Ashland, Ohio (Spring, 1980), p. 16.
6. Richard L. Pratt, Jr., *Every Thought Captive: A Study Manual for the Defense of Christian Truth* (Phillipsburg, NJ: Presbyterian and Reformed, 1979), p. 87.
7. R. C. Sproul, *The Psychology of Atheism* (Minneapolis, MN: Bethany Fellowship, 1974), pp. 128-29.
8. Bahnsen, "The Encounter of Jerusalem with Athens," p. 11.
9. Robert McCauley, "The Business of the University," *Liberal Education*, 68:1 (1982), p. 28.
10. David Chilton, *Paradise Restored: A Biblical Theology of Dominion* (Ft. Worth, TX: Dominion Press, [1985] 1987), p. 4.
11. John J. Dunphy, "A Religion for a New Age," *The Humanist* (January/February 1983), p. 26. Quoted in John W. Whitehead, *The Stealing of America* (Westchester, IL: Crossway Books, 1983), p. 95. Emphasis supplied.
12. From a letter to the author, April 27, 1979.
13. Herbert Schlossberg, *Idols for Destruction: Christian Faith and its Confrontation with American Society* (Wheaton, IL: Crossway Books, [1983] 1993).
14. Herman J. Muller, "One Hundred Years Without Darwin Are Enough," *The Humanist*, XIX (1959); reprinted in Philip Appleman, ed., *Darwin: A Norton Critical Edition* (New York: Norton, 1970), p. 570; quoted by Gary North, *The Dominion Covenant: Genesis* (2nd ed.; Tyler, TX: Institute for Christian Economics, [1982] 1987), p. 245.

Chapter 2 – Worldviews in Conflict

1. Harry Blamires, *The Christian Mind* (London: S.C.P.K., 1963), p. 3.
2. Joseph Epstein, "A Case of Academic Freedom," *Commentary* (September 1986), pp. 40-41.
3. Herbert Schlossberg and Marvin Olasky, *Turning Point: A Christian Worldview Declaration* (Westchester, IL: Crossway Books, 1987), p. 47.

END NOTES

4. The First Amendment addresses religion this way: "Congress shall make no law respecting an establishment of religion or prohibiting the free exercise thereof; or abridging the freedom of speech, or of the press; or the right of the people peaceably to assemble, and to petition the Government for a redress of grievances." Notice that there is no mention of a "separation between church and state."
5. W. Andrew Hoffecker, "Preface: Perspective and Method in Building a World View," *Building a Christian World View: God, Man, and Knowledge* (Phillipsburg, NJ: Presbyterian and Reformed, 1986), pp. ix-x.
6. Schlossberg and Olasky, *Turning Point*, p. 71.
7. John M. Frame, *The Doctrine of the Knowledge of God* (Phillipsburg, NJ: Presbyterian and Reformed, 1987), pp. 45, 125.
8. John W. Whitehead, *The End of Man* (Westchester, IL: Crossway, 1986), p. 16.
9. R. J. Rushdoony, *The Institutes of Biblical Law* (Phillipsburg, NJ: Presbyterian and Reformed, 1973), p. 540.
10. Thomas V. Morris, *Francis Schaeffer's Apologetics: A Critique* (Chicago, IL: Moody Press, 1976), p. 108n.
11. Whittaker Chambers, *Witness* (New York: Random House, 1952), pp. 9-10.
12. William L. Shirer, *The Rise and Fall of the Third Reich: A History of Nazi Germany* (New York: Simon and Schuster, 1960), p. 240.
13. William Shirer, *The Nightmare Years: 1930-1940* (Boston, MA: Little, Brown and Company, 1984), p. 156.
14. Donald D. Wall, "The Lutheran Response to the Hitler Regime in Germany," ed., Robert D. Linder, *God and Caesar: Case Studies in the Relationship Between Christianity and the State* (Longview, TX: The Conference on Faith and History, 1971), p. 88.
15. Shirer, *The Rise and Fall of the Third Reich*, pp. 248-49.
16. *Ibid.*, p. 249.
17. *Idem.*
18. Rheta Grimsley Johnson, "'People' vs. Fundamentalists," *The Marietta Daily Journal* (September 2, 1986), p. 4A.
19. A portion of a radio editorial heard over WGST Radio in Atlanta, Georgia on September 9, 1986.
20. "A Conversation With Francis Coppola," *U.S. News and World Report* (April 5, 1982), p. 68.
21. Alan N. Schoonmaker, *A Student's Survival Manual, or How to Get an Education Despite it All* (New York: Harper & Row, 1971), pp. 111-12.
22. Edmund W. Sinnott, *The Biology of the Spirit* (New York: The Viking Press, 1955), p. 7.
23. Whitehead, *The End of Man*, p. 144.
24. Charles B. Thaxton and Stephen C. Meyer, "Coming soon . . . human rights for bacteria?," *Houston Chronicle* (January 10, 1988), p. 4, section 6.
25. Lloyd Billingsley, *The Generation That Knew Not Josef: A Critique of Marxism and the Religious Left* (Portland, OR: Multnomah Press, 1985), p. 24.
26. *Idem.*

Chapter 3 – The Christian Worldview

1. John Calvin, *Institutes of the Christian Religion*, John T. McNeill, ed. (Philadelphia, PA: Westminster Press, 1960), Book I, chapter 2, section 1.
2. The Trinity is a difficult concept. It is not the purpose of this book to discuss the finer points of theology. This short definition defines the doctrine, although it does not fully explain it: "Within the one essence of the Godhead we have to distinguish

three 'persons' who are neither three gods on the one side, nor three parts or modes of God on the other, but coequally and coeternally God." Geoffrey W. Bromiley, "The Trinity," *Baker's Dictionary of Theology* (Grand Rapids, MI: Baker Book House, 1960), p. 531.
3. "God and Biblical Language," *God's Inerrant Word: An International Symposium on the Trustworthiness of Scripture*, John Warwick Montgomery, ed. (Minneapolis, MN: Bethany Fellowship, 1974), p. 173.
4. Conde Pallen, *Crucible Island* (New York, 1919), quoted in Thomas Molnar, *Utopia: The Perennial Heresy* (New York: Sheed and Ward, 1967), p. 186.
5. Francis Schaeffer, *The Complete Works of Francis A. Schaeffer: A Christian Worldview*, 5 vols.: *He Is There and He Is Not Silent* (Westchester, IL: Crossway Books, 1984), vol. 1, pp. 274-352.
6. James W. Sire, *The Universe Next Door: A Basic World View Catalog* (Downers Grove, IL: InterVarsity Press, 1976), pp. 35-36. An updated and expanded edition was published in 1988.
7. *Ibid.*, p. 37.
8. *Ibid.*, p. 49.
9. See John Eidsmoe, *Christianity and the Constitution* (Grand Rapids, MI: Baker Book House, 1987), pp. 39-45. "Deism, while it existed in America and was accepted by a few leading Americans (Thomas Paine, Ethan Allen, and possibly James Wilson), was (1) less influential than Christianity and (2) fundamentally compatible with Christianity in its view of law and government" (p. 45).
10. Carl Sagan, *Cosmos* (New York: Ballantine Books, [1980] 1985), p. 1.
11. Carl F. Ellis, Jr., *Beyond Liberation: The Gospel in the Black American Experience* (Downers Grove, IL: InterVarsity Press, 1983), p. 17.
12. Paul Kurtz, ed., *The Humanist Manifesto I and II* (Buffalo, NY: Prometheus Books, 1973), p. 16.
13. Arlie J. Hoover, *Dear Agnos: A Defense of Christianity* (Grand Rapids, MI: Baker Book House, 1976), p. 106.
14. *Life and Letters of Charles Darwin*, Frances Darwin, ed. (New York: Johnson Reprint), vol. 1, p. 285. Quoted in Hoover, *Dear Agnes*, pp. 106-107.
15. Robert A. Morey, *Death and the Afterlife* (Minneapolis, MN: Bethany House, 1984), p. 191.
16. Kurtz, ed., *Humanist Manifesto I and II*, p. 16.
17. *Ibid.*, p. 14.
18. Joseph Fletcher and John Warwick Montgomery, *Situation Ethics: True or False?: A Dialogue Between Joseph Fletcher and John Warwick Montgomery* (Minneapolis, MN: Bethany Fellowship, 1972), p. 15.
19. "Students Defend Abortion For 'High' Social Reasons," *The Rutherford Institute*, Vol. 1, No. 2 (January/February 1984), p. 8.
20. Friedrich Engels, *Anti-Dühring* (1934). Quoted in Francis Nigel Lee, *Communist Eschatology: A Christian Philosophical Analysis of the Post-Capitalistic Views of Marx, Engels and Lenin* (Nutley, NJ: The Craig Press, 1974), p. 322.
21. Sidney Abbott and Barbara Love, *Sappho Was a Right-On Woman: A Liberated View of Lesbianism* (New York: Stein and Day, 1972).
22. Adolf Hitler at Buckenburg, October 7, 1933; *cf. The Speeches of Adolf Hitler*, 1929-39, N. H. Baynes, ed. (2 vols., Oxford, 1942), vol. 1, pp. 871-72. Quoted in Leonard Peikoff, *The Ominous Parallels: The End of Freedom in America* (New York: Stein and Day, 1982), p. 3.
23. The Bible does not talk about rights. See Gary DeMar, *God and Government: The Restoration of the Republic* (Atlanta, GA: American Vision, 1986), pp. 212-43.
24. Naturalism as a philosophical system should not be confused with caring for the environment.

END NOTES

25. Rousas J. Rushdoony, *Salvation and Godly Rule* (Vallecito, CA: Ross House Books, 1983), p. 66.
26. Allan Bloom, *The Closing of the American Mind: How Higher Education Has Failed Democracy and Impoverished the Souls of Today's Students* (New York: Simon and Shuster, 1987), p. 25.
27. David Brock, "A Philosopher Hurls Down a Stinging Moral Gauntlet," *Insight* (May 11, 1987), p. 10.
28. It is true that language (as a social tool) is not used completely in the same way as in the 1780s. The issue, however, is whether the *sense* or *intent* of the words from the 1780s can be ascertained and understood effectively today.
29. John W. Whitehead, *The Second American Revolution* (Westchester, IL: Crossway Books, [1982] 1985), p. 46.
30. Os Guinness, *The Dust of Death: A Critique of the Establishment and the Counter Culture and a Proposal for a Third Way* (Downers Grove, IL: InterVarsity Press, 1973), p. 338. A revised edition was published by Crossway Books in 1994.
31. Stephen Jay Gould, "The Meaning of Life," *Life Magazine* (December 1988), p. 84.

Chapter 4 – Shopping for a God

1. John W. Whitehead, *The End of Man* (Westchester, IL: Crossway Books, 1986), p. 15.
2. Herbert Schlossberg, *Idols for Destruction: Christian Faith and Its Confrontation with American Society* (Wheaton, IL: Crossway Books, [1983] 1993), p. 6.
3. "Are American Families Finding New Strength in Spirituality?" *Better Homes and Gardens* (January 1988), p. 19. The editor of *Better Homes and Gardens*, David Jordan, was surprised by the response of the magazine's readership. He writes:

    I must admit that when our managing editor, Kate Greer, urged me to let her publish the questionnaire "Are American Families Finding New Strength in Spirituality?" in our September issue last year, I wasn't all that enthusiastic. . . .

    But now, the results are in, and I'm amazed. . . . I have to comment on two things: the size of the response (eighty thousand replies when we expected thirty thousand), and the fact that more than fifty percent of you said you thought spirituality is gaining influence on family life in America. These statistics illuminate a significant shift in the spiritual life of many of us (p. 15).

4. *Ibid.*, p. 25.
5. *Idem*.
6. Allan Bloom, *The Closing of the American Mind: How Higher Education Has Failed Democracy and Impoverished the Souls of Today's Students* (New York: Simon and Schuster, 1987), p. 26.
7. Douglas Groothuis, "The Smorgasbord Mentality," *Eternity* (May 1985), p. 32.
8. See Gary DeMar, *Ruler of the Nations* (Atlanta, GA: American Vision, 1987), pp. 22-23 and *God and Government: A Biblical and Historical Study* (Atlanta, GA: American Vision, 1990), p. 90 for a definition of "democracy" and its inherent instability.
9. Groothuis, "The Smorgasbord Mentality," p. 33.
10. While Mormons may accept the Bible as authoritative, they also maintain that *The Book of Mormon*, *The Pearl of Great Price*, *Doctrine and Covenants*, and the continuing authority of the church apostles are equally trustworthy and authoritative.
11. Quoted in John Allan, *Shopping for a God: Fringe Religions Today* (Grand Rapids, MI: Baker Book House, 1987), p. 10.
12. C. S. Lewis, *They Asked for a Paper* (London: Geoffrey Bles, 1962), pp. 164f.

13. John Frame, *The Doctrine of the Knowledge of God* (Phillipsburg, NJ: Presbyterian and Reformed, 1987), p. 258.
14. Thomas Sowell, *Knowledge and Decisions* (New York: Basic Books, 1980), p. 3.
15. J. P. Moreland, *Scaling the Secular City: A Defense of Christianity* (Grand Rapids, MI: Baker Book House, 1987), p. 190. The short story *Twelve Angry Men*, and later a movie starring Henry Fonda, depicts this process quite well.
16. "Modern irrationalism has not in the least encroached upon the domain of the intellect as the natural man thinks of it. Irrationalism has merely taken possession of that which the intellect, by its own admission, cannot in any case control. Irrationalism has a secret treaty with rationalism by which the former cedes to the latter so much of its territory as the latter can at any given time find the forces to control." Cornelius Van Til, *The Defense of the Faith* (rev. ed.; Philadelphia, PA: Presbyterian and Reformed, 1963), pp. 125-26.
17. Michael Denton, *Evolution: A Theory in Crisis* (Bethesda, MD: Adler & Adler, 1986), p. 255.
18. Edmund H. Harvey, ed., *Reader's Digest Book of Facts* (Pleasantville, NY: The Reader's Digest Association, Inc., 1987), pp. 388f.
19. Carl Sagan, *Cosmos* (New York: Ballantine Books, [1980] 1985), p. 1.
20. *Idem.*
21. *Ibid.*, pp. 241-42.
22. *Idem.*
23. *Ibid.*, p. 286.
24. *Ibid.*, p. 200.
25. *Idem.*
26. *Idem.*
27. *Ibid.*, p. 212.
28. Herman J. Muller, "One Hundred Years Without Darwinism Are Enough," *The Humanist*, XIX (1959); reprinted in Philip Appelman, ed., *Darwin: A Norton Critical Edition* (New York: Norton, 1970), p. 570.
29. Schlossberg, *Idols for Destruction*, p. 84.
30. Carl Sagan, *Broca's Brain: Reflections on the Romance of Science* (New York: Random House, 1979), p. 286.
31. These quotations are cited in Schlossberg, *Idols for Destruction*, pp. 2-3.

Chapter 5 – Leaping into the Void

1. Aldous Huxley, *Science, Liberty, and Peace* (New York: Harper, 1946), p. 291.
2. Herbert Schlossberg, *Idols for Destruction: Christian Faith and its Confrontation with American Society* (Wheaton, IL: Crossway Books, [1983] 1993), p. 2.
3. *Idem.*
4. John R. Robbins, "The Scientist as Evangelist," *Trinity Review* (The Trinity Foundation, P.O. Box 169, Jefferson, MD 21755, January-February 1986), p. 3.
5. R. L. Meek, ed., *Marx and Engels on Malthus* (New York: International Publishers, 1954), p. 171. Quoted in Michael Pitman, *Adam and Evolution* (London, England: Rider & Company, 1984), p. 24.
6. *Idem.*
7. John Jefferson Davis, *Foundations of Evangelical Theology* (Grand Rapids, MI: Baker Book House, 1984), p. 127.
8. Francis A. Schaeffer, *The Complete Works of Francis Schaeffer: A Christian Worldview*, 5 vols.: *Escape From Reason* (Westchester, IL: Crossway Books, 1984), vol. 1, pp. 237-38.

END NOTES

9. Pat Means, *The Mystical Maze* (San Bernardino, CA: Campus Crusade for Christ, 1976), p. 39.
10. James W. Sire, *The Universe Next Door: A Basic World View Catalog* (Downers Grove, IL: InterVarsity Press, 1976), p. 133. An updated and expanded edition was published in 1988.
11. Pagan creation myths abound with this notion. According to one Babylonian account, Marduk, the great stone god, "killed the dragon Tiamat and split her body in half. The upper half was made into the sky, and the lower half the earth." John J. Davis, *Paradise to Prison: Studies in Genesis* (Grand Rapids, MI: Baker Book House, 1975), p. 69.
12. Douglas R. Groothuis, *Unmasking the New Age: Is There a New Religious Movement Trying to Transform Society?* (Downers Grove, IL: InterVarsity Press, 1986), p. 18.
13. Means, *The Mystical Maze*, p. 21.
14. Groothuis, *Unmasking the New Age*, p. 21.
15. *Idem*.
16. "The universe was conceived as a 'great chain of Being,' starting with the completely real being, the One, or God, or the Idea of the Good, whose very nature overflowed into lesser realms of being, such as the world of Ideas, human beings, animals, inanimate objects, down to matter, 'the last faint shadow of reality. . . .'

    "In this theory, the aim of human existence was seen as an attempt to move up the ladder of existence, to become more real. To accomplish this, men were to direct their interests and attention to what was above them on the 'great chain of Being.' By philosophizing they could liberate themselves from the sense world, and become more and more part of the intelligible world. The more one could understand, the more one would become like what one understood. Ultimately, if successful, one would reach the culmination of the 'journey of the mind of God,' by a mystical union with the One. Thus the final end of seeking to understand the nature of reality would be to become absorbed by what is most real, and to lose all of one's individuality which merely represents lesser degrees of reality. Through philosophizing, through art, and through mystic experience of unity with the One, [an individual found] the path to human salvation, and of liberation from the lesser reality of sensory and material worlds." Avrum Stroll and Richard H. Popkin, *Introduction to Philosophy* (2nd ed.; New York: Holt, Rhinehart and Winston, 1972), pp. 100-101.
17. Ray Sutton, *That You May Prosper: Dominion By Covenant* (Tyler, TX: Dominion Press, 1987), p. 37.
18. For an insightful analysis and critique of Cayce's views see: Gary North, *Unholy Spirits: Occultism and New Age Humanism* (Ft. Worth, TX: Dominion Press, 1986), pp. 193-225. Cayce was an avid Bible student. It is reported that he tried to read through the Bible once each year. He tried to reconcile his occultism with the Bible and failed, ignoring Hebrews 9:26-27. See Phillip J. Swihart, *Reincarnation, Edgar Cayce & the Bible* (Downers Grove, IL: InterVarsity Press, 1975).
19. John Snyder, *Reincarnation vs. Resurrection* (Chicago, IL: Moody Press, 1984), p. 19.
20. Naisbitt, *Megatrends: Ten New Directions Transforming Our Lives* (New York: Warner Books, 1982). Marilyn Ferguson, author of *The Aquarian Conspiracy*, writes of *Megatrends*: "In such turbulent times, we prize those among us who see clearly. John Naisbitt offers a dramatic, convincing view on the changes already under way. This is a book for everyone who wants a sense of the near future."
21. John Naisbitt and Patricia Aburdene, *Re-inventing the Corporation* (New York: Warner Books, 1985), p. 252.
22. New York: Dell, 1979.
23. New York: Simon and Schuster, 1982.

24. Los Angeles, CA: J. P. Tarcher, Inc., 1980.
25. North, *Unholy Spirits*, p. 6.
26. Schaeffer, *The Complete Works of Francis A. Schaeffer*, 5 vols.: *Pollution and the Death of Man: The Christian View of Ecology*, vol. 5, pp. 3-76.
27. "New Age Harmonies," *Time* (December 7, 1987), p. 72.
28. Os Guinness, *The Dust of Death: A Critique of the Establishment and the Counter Culture—and a Proposal for a Third Way* (Downers Grove, IL: InterVarsity Press, 1973), p. 209. A revised edition was published by Crossway Books in 1994.
29. *Idem.*
30. *Idem.*
31. For helpful and balanced treatments of the New Age movement see: Gary DeMar and Peter J. Leithart, *The Reduction of Christianity: A Biblical Response to Dave Hunt* (Ft. Worth, TX: Dominion Press, 1988); Karen Hoyt, ed., *The New Age Rage: A Probing Analysis of The Newest Religious Craze* (Old Tappan, NJ: Fleming H. Revell Company, 1987); Douglas R. Groothuis, *Unmasking the New Age: Is There a New Religious Movement Trying to Transform Society?* (Downers Grove, IL: InterVarsity Press, 1986).
32. Stephen H. Balch and Herbert I. London, "The Tenured Left," *Commentary* (October 1986), pp. 44-45.
33. Quoted in *ibid.*, p. 45.
34. Quoted in *ibid.*
35. Karl Marx, "Contribution to the Critique of Hegel's Philosophy of Right," in *Early Writings*, trans. and ed. by T. B. Bottomore (New York: McGraw-Hill, 1963), pp. 43-44.
36. Klaus Bockmuehl, *The Challenge of Marxism: A Christian Response* (Downers Grove, IL: InterVarsity Press, 1980), p. 52.
37. Quoted in *ibid.*, p. 91.
38. Emilio A. Núñez C., *Liberation Theology*, trans. by Paul E. Sywulka (Chicago, IL: Moody Press, 1985), p. 47.
39. *Ibid.*, p. 205.
40. *Ibid.*, pp. 235-36.
41. *Ibid.*, p. 236.
42. *Ibid.*, p. 273.
43. Harold O. J. Brown, "What Is Liberation Theology?" in *Liberation Theology*, Ronald Nash, ed. (Milford, MI: Mott Media, 1984), p. 11.
44. D. G. Myers, "MLA Malaise," *The American Spectator*, (March 1988), p. 33.
45. James L. Sauer, "Letter From Philadelphia," *Chronicles* (February 1988), pp. 40-41.
46. Phyllis Zagano, "In Whose Image?—Feminist Theology at the Crossroads," *This World* (Fall 1986), pp. 81, 83-84.
47. Jeffrey B. Russell, *A History of Witchcraft* (London: Thames and Hudson, 1980), p. 156.
48. Quoted in Mary Pride, *The Way Home: Beyond Feminism, Back to Reality* (Westchester, IL: Crossway, 1985), p. 5.
49. George Gilder, *Men and Marriage* (Gretna, LA: Pelican, 1986), pp. 103-104.
50. Quoted in Mary Pride, *The Way Home*, p. 12.
51. Allan Bloom, *The Closing of the American Mind: How Higher Education Has Failed Democracy and Impoverished the Souls of Today's Students* (New York: Simon and Schuster, 1987).
52. Quoted in Bernard D. N. Grebanier, *English Literature*, 2 vols. (Woodbury, NY: Baron's Educational Series), vol. 2, p. 627.
53. Bloom, *Closing of the American Mind*, p. 256.

---END NOTES---

54. David Cohen, "Behaviorism," in *The Oxford Companion to the Mind*, Richard L. Gregory, ed. (New York: Oxford University Press, 1987), p. 71.
55. B. F. Skinner, "Skinner on Behaviorism," in *ibid.*, p. 75.
56. *Ibid.*
57. Vincent Bugliosi, *Helter Skelter: The True Story of the Manson Murders* (New York: W. W. Norton & Company, 1974), p. 389.
58. *Ibid.*, p. 224.

Chapter 6 – Spiritual Counterfeits

1. Murray N. Rothbard, *The Sociology of the Ayn Rand Cult* (Port Townsend, WA: Liberty Publishing, 1987), p. 1.
2. J. K. Van Baalen, "The Unpaid Bills of the Church," in *Chaos of Cults* (4th ed.; Grand Rapids, MI: Eerdmans, 1962), pp. 390-98.
3. Mary Baker Eddy, *Christian Science Journal*, January 1901. Quoted in Josh McDowell and Don Stewart, *Handbook of Today's Religions* (San Bernardino, CA: Here's Life Publishers, 1983), p. 123.
4. Quoted in *ibid.*, p. 37.
5. Herbert W. Armstrong, *The Autobiography of Herbert W. Armstrong* (Pasadena, CA: Ambassador College Press, 1967), p. 298-99. Quoted in McDowell and Stewart, *Handbook of Today's Religions*, p. 114.
6. Vincent Bugliosi, *Helter Skelter: The True Story of the Manson Murders* (New York: W. W. Norton and Company, 1974), p. 428. As a follow-up, the prosecuting attorney asked these two questions:
    Q. "Even commit murder?" I asked instantly.
    A. "I'd do anything for God."
    Q. "Including murder?" I pressed.
    A. "That's right. If I believed it was right" (p. 429).
7. Mary Baker Eddy, *Science and Health with Key to the Scriptures* (Boston, MA: The First Church of Christ, Scientist, 1971), p. 480.
8. William Sanford LaSor, *The Truth About Armageddon: What the Bible Says About the End Times* (Grand Rapids, MI: Baker Book House, 1982), p. 103, Note *a*. For a balanced treatment of what Christians should expect in terms of the "end times," the reader is encouraged to study Gary DeMar, *Last Days Madness: Obsession of the Modern Church* (Atlanta, GA: American Vision, 1994).

Chapter 7 – The Occult Explosion

1. C. S. Lewis, *The Screwtape Letters* (New York: Macmillan, [1942] 1946), p. 9.
2. "Theologian Protests 'Witchcraft at Indiana University,'" *Christian News* (May 18, 1987), p. 1.
3. "Cobb Teen Charged in 'Ritual Murder' of Girl, 15," *The Marietta Daily Journal* (January 29, 1988), p. 7A.
4. Dirk Kinnane Roelofsma, "Battling Satanism a Haunting Task," *Insight* (January 11, 1988), p. 49.
5. *Idem.*
6. Gary North, *Unholy Spirits: Occultism and New Age Humanism* (Ft. Worth, TX: Dominion Press, 1986), pp. 65-66.

7. It's ironic that Roman Polanski directed *Rosemary's Baby*. Sharon Tate, the victim of Charles Manson's murdering occult-worshipping "Family," was pregnant at the time of her slaughter. She was married to Roman Polanski. Sharon Tate's movie debut was *Eye of the Devil* (1965), in which she "played a country girl with bewitching powers." In the film, David Niven "became the victim of a hooded cult which practiced ritual sacrifice." Vincent Bugliosi, *Helter Skelter: The True Story of the Manson Murders* (New York: W. W. Norton, 1974), p. 27. In 1967 Sharon Tate appeared in another Polanski Production, *The Fearless Vampire Killers*. "A victim of the vampire early in the picture, in the last scene she bites her lover, Polanski, creating still another monster" (p. 28).
8. Robert S. Wheeler, *The Children of Darkness: Some Heretical Reflections on the Kid Cult* (New Rochelle, NY: Arlington House, 1973), p. 31.
9. James Sire, *The Universe Next Door: A Basic World View Catalog* (Downers Grove, IL: InterVarsity Press, 1976), p. 142.
10. Gary DeMar and Peter J. Leithart, *The Reduction of Christianity: A Biblical Response to Dave Hunt* (Ft. Worth, TX: Dominion Press, 1988).
11. Os Guinness, *The Dust of Death: A Critique of the Establishment and the Counter Culture – and a Proposal for a Third Way* (Downers Grove, IL: InterVarsity Press, 1973), p. 277. A revised edition was published by Crossway Books in 1994.
12. Cornelius Van Til, *The Defense of the Faith* (3rd. ed.; Phillipsburg, NJ: Presbyterian and Reformed, 1967), p. 8.
13. Jeffrey B. Russell, *A History of Witchcraft: Sorcerers, Heretics and Pagans* (London: Thames and Hudson, 1980), pp. 174-75.
14. Quoted in Chris Morgan and David Langford, *Facts and Fallacies: A Book of Definitive Mistakes and Misguided Predictions* (Ontario, Canada: John Wiley & Sons Canada Limited, 1981), p. 110.
15. Guinness, *The Dust of Death*, p. 280.
16. Peter Leithart and George Grant, *A Christian Response to Dungeons & Dragons: The Catechism of the Occult* (Ft. Worth, TX: Dominion Press, 1987), p. 7.
17. Robert A. Morey, *Horoscopes and the Christian* (Minneapolis, MN: Bethany House, 1981).
18. Robert Somerlott, *"Here, Mr. Splitfoot": An Informal Exploration into Modern Occultism* (New York: Viking, 1971), p. 4.
19. Leithart and Grant, *A Christian Response to Dungeons & Dragons*, p. 4.
20. Quoted in *ibid.*, p. 7.
21. Josh McDowell and Don Stewart, *Handbook of Today's Religions* (San Bernardino, CA: Here's Life Publishers, 1983), p. 150.
22. Gary North, *Unholy Spirits*, p. 65.
23. Quoted in John M. Leighty, "Biblical Satan is Lukewarm Topic in Today's Modern World," *The Marietta Daily Journal* (January 29, 1988), p. 5B.
24. James Randi, *Flim-Flam: Psychics, ESP, Unicorns and other Delusions* (Buffalo, NY: Prometheus Books, [1982] 1987), pp. 248-49. See his chapter on "Medical Humbugs," pp. 173-95. For a Christian critique of the paranormal, see Danny Korem and Paul Meier, *The Fakers: Exploding the Myths of the Supernatural* (Grand Rapids, MI: Baker Book House, [1980] 1981).
25. Korem and Meier, *The Fakers*, p. 17. Korem illustrates his point by convincing a student at Tulane University that he, Korem, has supernatural powers and that he is a visitor from the planet Pluto.
26. Milbourne Christopher, *Houdini: The Untold Story* (New York: Pocket Books, [1969] 1975), p. 215.
27. Quoted in Loraine Boettner, *Immortality* (Philadelphia, PA: Presbyterian and Reformed, 1956), p. 156.
28. Bill Kelley, "Horror Comes to TV," *The Marietta Daily Journal* (October 10, 1988).

END NOTES

Chapter 8 – Living in a Postmodern World

1. David F. Wells, *God in the Wasteland: The Reality of Truth in a World of Fading Dreams* (Grand Rapids, MI: Eerdmans, 1994), p. 48.
2. George Barna, *Absolute Confusion: How our Moral and Spiritual Foundations Are Eroding in this Age of Change* (Ventura, CA: Regal Books, 1993).
3. For a more detailed examination of the many issues raised by postmodern thought, see Stephen Best and Douglas Kellner, *Postmodern Theory: Critical Interrogations* (New York: The Guilford Press, 1991); Stephen Connor, *Postmodernist Culture: An Introduction to Theories of the Contemporary* (Cambridge, MA: Basil Blackwell, 1989); Jean-François Lyotard, *The Postmodern Condition: A Report on Knowledge*, trans. Geoff Bennington and Brian Massumi (Manchester: Manchester University Press, 1984). From a Christian point of view see Gene Edward Veith, *Postmodern Times: A Christian Guide to Contemporary Thought and Culture* (Wheaton, IL: Crossway Books, 1994).
4. Veith, *Postmodern Times*, p. 19. Worldview shifts are more fully explained and documented in Richard Tarnas, *The Passion of the Western Mind: Understanding the Ideas that Have Shaped Our Worldview* (New York: Harmony Books, 1991).
5. Veith, *Postmodern Times*, p. 29.
6. See William H. Halverson, *A Concise Introduction to Philosophy*, 4th ed. (New York: McGraw-Hill Publishers, 1981), pp. 413-17. Halverson points out that the study of philosophy encompasses all other disciplines. It seeks to create the concepts which will unify knowledge and provide a foundation for meaning.
7. Thomas C. Oden, *Two Worlds: Notes on the Death of Modernity in America and Russia* (Downers Grove, IL: InterVarsity Press, 1992), p. 32.
8. James Turner, *Without God, Without Creed: The Origins of Unbelief in America* (Baltimore, MD: Johns Hopkins University Press, 1985), p. 36.
9. *Idem.*
10. *Idem.*
11. For a detailed account of positivism, see Michael Corrado, *The Analytic Tradition in Philosophy: Background and Issues* (Chicago: American Library Association, 1975).
12. See Gary Scott Smith, "Naturalistic Humanism," in *Building a Christian Worldview: God, Man, and Knowledge*, eds. Andrew Hoffecker and Gary Scott Smith (Phillipsburg, NJ: Presbyterian and Reformed, 1986), pp. 161-81.
13. See Edward J. Young, *An Introduction to the Old Testament* (Grand Rapids: Eerdmans, [1949] 1977), pp. 123-41. In responding to the charge that Christianity and reason are at odds with each other, Young says, "Christianity and reason, of course, are not enemies, for Christianity is the only *reasonable* explanation of life, and true reason, which is derived from God, is both humble and receptive."
14. Diogenes Allen, *Christian Faith in a Postmodern World: The Full Wealth of Conviction* (Louisville, KY: Westminster/John Knox, 1989), p. 36.
15. Stephen Best and Douglas Kellner, *Postmodern Theory: Critical Interrogations* (New York: The Guilford Press, 1991), p. 2.
16. See Thomas Kuhn, *The Structure of Scientific Revolutions* (Chicago, IL: The University of Chicago Press, 1970). Kuhn argues that scientists interpret the facts they observe according to their presuppositions about the nature of reality and knowledge.
17. Paul Johnson, *Modern Times: From the Twenties to the Nineties*, rev. ed. (New York: HarperCollins, 1991), p. 700.
18. With the developments in Einstein's relativity, Bohr's quantum mechanics, and Heisenburg's "Uncertainty Principle," strict Newtonian Determinism in physics was called into question. Subatomic particles didn't seem to follow the physical patterns of their constructs. At times they behaved like particles, and at other times

they behaved like waves. In Kuhnian terms, "Normal science" was not able to account for these anomalies. In the words of Sir James Jeans, the "physical world of twentieth-century physics did not look like a great machine as it did a great thought" (Richard Tarnas, *The Passion of the Western Mind*, p. 356).
19. Herbert Kohl, *From Archetype to Zeitgeist: Powerful Ideas for Powerful Thinking* (Boston, MA: Little, Brown and Company, 1992), p. 127.
20. Tarnas, *The Passion of the Western Mind*, *p*. 396. Emphasis added.
21. This process of the reduction of man is described in excellent detail in William Barrett, *Death of the Soul: From Descartes to the Computer* (New York: Anchor/Doubleday, 1986).
22. Phillip E. Johnson, "The Modernist Impasse in Law," in *God and Culture: Essays in Honor of Carl F. H. Henry*, eds. D. A. Carson and John D. Woodbridge (Grand Rapids, MI: Eerdmans, 1993), pp. 180-94.
23. Gary North, *Unholy Spirits: Occultism and New Age Humanism* (Tyler, TX: Dominion Press, 1986), p. 22.
24. Herbert Schlossberg, *Idols for Destruction: The Conflict of Christian Faith and American Culture* (Wheaton, IL: Crossway Books, [1983] 1993), p. 2.
25. *Idem.*
26. *Idem.*
27. "The phenomenon we call 'the Sixties' did not begin at 12:01 A.M. on January 1, 1960. It is not a chronological entity so much as a cultural or mythic one. Even if we identify the myth with the decade, it would be more accurate to say that it began on November 8, 1960, with the election of John F. Kennedy, and ended May 4, 1970, on the campus of Kent State" when National Guardsmen killed four students as a crowd gathered to protest escalation of United States military policy in Vietnam. Annie Gottlieb, *Do You Believe in Magic?: The Second Coming of the 60's Generation* (New York: Random House/Times Books, 1987), p. 17.
28. Quoted in *ibid.*, p. 18.
29. *Idem.*
30. North, *Unholy Spirits*, p. 23.
31. Gottlieb, *Do You Believe in Magic?*, p. 47.
32. Quoted in *ibid.*, p. 18.
33. David Halberstam, *The Best and the Brightest* (New York: Random House, 1972).
34. Stephen Connor, *Postmodernist Culture: An Introduction to Theories of the Contemporary* (Cambridge, MA: Basil Blackwell, 1989), p. 6. Postmodernism was becoming more and more concrete, but modernism was still flourishing. It was the fall of communism in 1989 that drove the nail into the coffin of modernism.
35. At this point it is important to distinguish between *postmodern* and *postmodernism*. *Postmodern* refers to a period of time, whereas *postmodernism* refers to a distinct ideology. As Veith points out, "If the *modern* era is over, we are all postmodern, even though we reject the tenets of postmoder*nism*" (Veith, *Postmodern Times*, p. 42).
36. Gottlieb, *Do You Believe in Magic?*, p. 138.
37. Veith, *Postmodern Times*, p. 49.
38. Nihilism is the view that human existence is totally and irremediably meaningless, that nothing in the world has any value. The most obvious example of nihilism is found in the works of Friedrich Nietzsche (See Halverson, *A Concise Introduction to Philosophy*, pp. 448, 457-62).
39. Charles Mackenzie, "Kant's Copernican Revolution," in *Building a Christian Worldview*, 1:284 (emphasis added).
40. Veith, *Postmodern Times*, p. 57.
41. Dennis Farney, "Natural Questions," *Wall Street Journal* (July 11, 1994), p. A4.

END NOTES

42. Diogenes Allen, *Christian Belief in a Postmodern World*, p. 2.
43. *Ibid.*, p. 5.
44. Veith, *Postmodern Times*, pp. 20-23.
45. Cornelius Van Til, *An Introduction to Systematic Theology* (Philadelphia: den Dulk Foundation, 1974), p. 256.
46. Genesis 1:28.

Conclusion

1. William R. Fix, *The Bone Peddlers: Selling Evolution* (New York: Macmillan, 1984), p. xix.
2. William H. Halverson, *A Concise Introduction to Philosophy*, 3rd ed. (New York: Random House, 1976), p. 384. Quoted in Ronald H. Nash, *Faith and Reason: Searching for a Rational Faith* (Grand Rapids, MI: Zondervan/Academie, 1988), p. 46.
3. George M. Marston, *The Voice of Authority* (Nutley, NJ: Presbyterian and Reformed, 1960), p. xv.
4. Quoted in James Burke, *The Day the Universe Changed* (Boston, MA: Little, Brown and Company, 1985), p. 265.
5. *Idem.*
6. *Ibid.*, p. 266.
7. *Ibid.*, p. 265.
8. *Ibid.*, p. 273.
9. Quoted in John W. Whitehead, *The End of Man* (Westchester, IL: Crossway Books, 1986), p. 53.
10. Quoted in Burke, *The Day the Universe Changed*, p. 271.
11. Taken from the official records of masonic meetings at the International Congress at Paris, 1901. Quoted in H. Daniel-Rops, *A Fight for God: 1870-1939*, trans. John Warrington (London: J. M. Dent & Sons Ltd., [1963] 1966), pp. 8-9.
12. "O God, I am thinking thy thoughts after thee." Quoted in Charles E. Hummell, *The Galileo Connection: Resolving Conflicts between Science and the Bible* (Downers Grove, IL: InterVarsity Press, 1986), p. 57.
13. Daniel-Rops, *A Fight for God*, pp. 10-11.
14. Norman E. Harper, *Making Disciples: The Challenge of Christian Education at the End of the 20th Century* (Atlanta, GA: American Vision, 1981), p. 1.
15. Quoted in Daniel-Rops, *A Fight for God*, p. 18.
16. Quoted in *ibid.*, p. 18.
17. Rousas J. Rushdoony, *The Word of Flux: Modern Man and the Problem of Knowledge* (Fairfax, VA: Thoburn Press, 1975), p. 36.
18. John Jefferson Davis, *Foundations of Evangelical Theology* (Grand Rapids, MI: Baker Book House, 1984), p. 130.

NAME INDEX

Abbot, Edwin, 53-54
Allen, Diogenes, 135
Ammon, Otto, 146
Aquinas, Thomas, 133
Archimedes, 145
Aristotle, 45, 133
Armstrong, Herbert W., 107-8
Arnold, Matthew, 97-98
Atlas, 145
Augustine, 133

Bahnsen, Greg L., 16-17
Baum, Frank, 117
Barna, George, 131-32
Bennett, William, 90, 97
Berg, David Brandt, 108, 112
Bismarck, Otto von, 147
Bloom, Allan, 97, 98
Buddha, 67
Burrows, Robert J. L., 88

Caiphas, 11
Calvin, John, 133
Carnegie, Andrew, 147
Casteneda, Carlos, 124
Cayce, Edgar, 87
Chesterton, G. K., 25
Colero, Adolfo, 28
Copernicus, Nicolaus, 35
Coppola, Francis Ford, 37-38

Darwin, Charles, 56, 73, 137, 146-47
David, King, 15, 82
de Sade, Marquis, 57
Descartes, Rene, 5
Disney, Walt, 117

Dixon, Jeanne, 122
Dostoevsky, Fyodor, 88
Doyle, Arthur Conan, 126-27

Eddy, Mary Baker, 105, 108
Engels, Friedrich, 58, 82
Epstein, Joseph, 28
Erhard, Werner, 86, 108

Farrow, Mia, 117
Ferguson, Marilyn, 87, 89
Feuerbach, Ludwig, 148
Fillmore, Charles Sherlock, 108
Foley, Barbara, 28

Ford, Henry, 56
Frame, John M., 46

Gagarin, Yuri, 62
Gibbon, Edward, 134
Gilder, George, 96-97
Gould, Stephen Jay, 62-63
Guiness, Os, 88-89, 119

Haeckel, Ernst, 146
Harrison, George, 85, 88
Heinrich, Ernst, 148
Hitler, Adolf, 36, 82
Hodge, A. A., xii
Holmes, Sherlock, 126-27
Houdini, Harry, 127-28
Hume, David, 134
Huxley, Aldous, 37
Huxley, Julian, 61

Johnson, Lyndon B., 138

Johnson, Phillip, 136
Jones, Jim, 69-70, 109, 126

Karloff, Boris, 128-29
Kennedy, John F., 137-38
Kennedy, Robert, 138
Kepler, Johannes, 134, 147
King, Martin Luther, 138
King, Stephen, 128-29
Korem, Danny, 126
Kristol, Irving, 142

La Vey, Anton Szandor, 125
Lennon, John, 85
Lewis, C. S., 69, 117, 123
Lewontin, Richard, 90
Luther, Martin, 133

MacKenzie, Charles, 140
MacLaine, Shirley, 45, 87
Manson, Charles, 85, 101, 109, 116, 117
Marx, Karl, 82, 90-92, 146-47
Maupin, Bill, 112
McCartney, Paul, 85
McDowell, Josh, 28
Milton, John, 125
Mohammed, 67
Mollenkott, Virginia Ramey, 94-95
Montesquieu, 134
Moon, Sun Myung, 104, 108
Ms. Budapest, 115

Naisbitt, John, 87
Nathan the Prophet, 15
Nunez, Emilio A., 92-93

Pallen, Conde, 48-49
Pascal, Blaise, 76, 133
Paul the Apostle, 12-17
Pavlov, Ivan, 98-99
Peters, Ted, xi
Plato, 12, 97, 133
Ptolemaeus, Claudius, 133-34
Pulling, Patricia, 116

Ramirez, Richard, 115, 116
Reagan, Ronald, 97

Reuther, Rosemary Radford, 95
Rhodes, Frank H. T., 60-61
Rockefeller, John D., 147
Rogers, Will, 71
Roszak, Theodore, 83
Rousseau, Jean-Jacques, 97
Rushdoony, R. J., 33, 149
Russell, Bertrand, 121
Russell, Charles Taze, 108

Sagan, Carl, 53, 54, 74-77, 78
Santayana, George, 56
Satin, Mark, 87
Schlossberg, Herbert, 65
Scott, George C., 125
Shankar, Ravi, 88
Shirer, William, 36
Simpson, Gregory, 116
Skinner, B. F., 99-100
Smith, Adam, 134
Smith, Jim, 138
Smith, Joseph, 108
Socrates, 12
Solzhenitsyn, Aleksandr, 42
Spelling, Aaron, 128-29
Stalin, Josef, 82
Sutton, Ray R., 86
Suzuki, D. T., 84
Swami Muktananda, 86

Terry, Maury, 116

Veith, Gene, 132, 133, 142
Voltaire, 134
von Daniken, Erik, 34, 74

Watson, John B., 98, 99
Weaver, Mary Jo, 95
Webster, Daniel, 117
Welles, Orson, ix-x
Wells, H. G., x, 78, 81, 137
Wesley, John, 121
Wierwille, Victor Paul, 108
Winthrop, Robert C., 43

Yogi, Maharishi, 85

SUBJECT INDEX

Absolutes, 17, 73
Abortion, 10, 25, 34, 57, 60, 67, 77
AIDS, 77
Adam and Eve, 50
The American Scholar, 28
Angel on My Shoulder, 117
Apologetics, 8-19
   Definition, 9, 11-12
   Jesus, 10-11
   Paul the Apostle, 12-17
   Regeneration, 16
   Socrates, 12
Aquarian Conspiracy, The, 87, 89
Artist Class, 37-38
Astral Projection, 124
Astrology, 121, 122, 124
Atheism, 23, 40
   Consequences, 42-43
   See also Humanism; Naturalism; Materialism; Secularism
Athenian Philosophers, 13-17
Autonomy, 72
   Definition, 14

Baptists, 67
Basic Commitments, 31
   See also Presupposition; Worldview
Beatles, 85, 88
Behaviorism, 98-100
Bestiality, 58
Better Homes and Gardens, 66
Bible, 9, 25, 30, 43
   Authority, 120
   Special Revelation, 50
   Weapon, 7-10
Big Brother, 37

The Book of Mormon, 104
Bothered About Dungeons and Dragons (BADD), 116
Brainwashing, 38-39
Bride of Frankenstein, 129
Brown University, 147
Buddhism, 67, 68
   Zen Buddhism, 84

Canaanite Religion, 121
Carrie, 128
Celts, 121
Central Intelligence Agency (CIA), 28
"Chain of Being," 86
Chance, 55
Channelling, 66
Chariots of the Gods, 74
Child Abuse, 116
Children of God, 105, 108, 112
Chinese Communism, 38-39, 82
Christian Reformed, 67
Christian Science, 67, 104-5, 108, 109
Christianity,
   Defense, 8-10, 12-17
   Privatized, 24, 29, 37
   Public Education, 21
Church of Satan, 125
Civil Rights Movement, 37
Classical Education, 97-98
Copernican revolution, 133-34
Copernicus, Nicolaus, 134
Commentary, 28
Communism, 82, 135
   Christianity, 35
   See also Marxism
Cornell University, 60

Cosmos, 53, 74-76
Creation, 45, 50
Creation-evolution Debate, 10, 28
Creator-creature Distinction, 85, 86
Crystal Balls, 124
Cults, 103-10

DNA, 40
Damien — The Omen II, 117
Darwinism, 2, 61, 82, 136, 137, 146-47, 148
   See also Evolution; Darwin, Charles
Death, 56, 78
Declaration of Geneva, 60
Declaration of Independence (1776), 58
Declaration of the Rights of Man (1789), 59
Dehumanization, 19, 41-42, 57, 77
Deism, 52-53, 134
Demythologization, 119-20
Democracy, 67
Demon Seed, 117
The Devil and Daniel Webster, 117
Dialectical Materialism, 91
Divine Principle, 104
Doctrine and Covenants, 104
Dogma, 17-18
Dungeons and Dragons, 116, 121, 123, 124
The Dust of Death, 88-89

Eastern Religions, 84-89, 105
Egyptian Religion, 121
End of the World, 112
Enlightenment, the, 1, 98, 132, 133, 142, 146
Environmentalism, 59, 77, 101
Epicureans, 13
Epistemology
   Definition, 7
   See also Presupposition; Worldview; Apologetics
Equal Rights Amendment, 94, 96
Est, 86, 108
Eternal Life, 66
Evidence, 34-35, 40
   See also Neutrality

Evolution, 40, 41, 55, 72
Existentialism, 83
The Exorcist, 118
Extra-Sensory Perception (ESP), 124
Extra-Terrestrial Life, 72-77

Faith, 22
   See also Presupposition; Worldview
Fall of Man, 50
Fantasy Role Playing Games, 123
Feminism, 94-97, 141
The Final Conflict, 117
Flatland, 53-54
The Flim-Flam Man, 125
Fortune Telling, 124
Forum (formerly est), 86, 108
Frankenstein, 129
French Revolution, 2, 133
Friday the 13th: The Series, 128, 129
Fundamentalism, 66

Galileo, 134
General Assembly of the World Medical Organization, 60
General Revelation, 49
God
   Attributes, 45-47
   Creator, 45
   Father, 46
   Immanence, 46
   Judge, 15
   Lord, 46
   Omniscience, 47
   Person, 45-46, 85
   Sovereignty, 14-15
   Transcendence, 15, 46
   Triune, 45-46
God is Dead "Theology," 82-83
Gods from Outer Space, 74
Gold of the Gods, The, 74
Gospel, 16
Greece
   Philosophers, 13
   State religious, 12
Greenpeace, 77
Group Bonding, 111
Guilt, 15

SUBJECT INDEX

Gulag Archipelago, The, 42
Gulag, 82
Guyana, South America, 68, 126

Halloween, 129
Hare Krishna, 84, 85, 105
Harvard University, 60, 63
Heaven, 66
Hebraism, 98
Hedonism, 57
Hell, 66
Hellenism, 98
Helter Skelter, 85
Hinduism, 84, 109
Hippocratic Oath, 60
History, 56
Holocaust, 36
Holy Spirit, 16, 19-20, 21
Homosexuality, 58, 67, 77, 141
Horror Movies, 128
Human Rights, 58-59
Humanism, 2-3, 22-23, 25, 134-35, 148
   Definition, 21
   Naturalism, 55, 135
   New Age, 87-89
   Pessimism, 78-79, 135-36
   See also Naturalism; Materialism; Secularism
Humanist Manifesto II, 57
Hypnotism, 124

"I Am the Walrus," 85
Ideas, 32
Idolatry, 25
Image of God, 19, 41-42, 47-49
   Restored, 51
Immanence
   Definition, 46
   Transcendence, 46
In Search of Ancient Gods, 74
Indiana University, 115
Information Overload, 111
Information Society, 87
Intellectual Warfare, 5-10, 17-19, 25, 27, 39
International Committee Against Racism (InCAR), 28

Invisible Man, The, 78
Irrationalism, 72-77, 83
   Satanism, 116
   See also Rationalism; Occult; Cults
Irrationality, 68-70
Islam, 105

Jehovah's Witnesses, 104, 105, 108, 111-12
Jesus Christ
   Cults, 50
   Deity, 34-35, 106-7
   Incarnation and Revelation, 50
   Return, 112-13
Jonestown, 68-70
Judgment, 15-16, 17

Karma, 85, 101
Kent State University, 139
Knowledge
   Divine and Human, 47, 48
   Unbeliever's, 49
   Uncertainty, 56
   Unity, 33

LaBianca Murders, 85
Latin America, 94
Leninism, 82
Lesbianism, 58
Liberation Theology, 92-94
Lighthouse Gospel Tract Foundation, 112
"Love Bombing," 111

Magic, 124
Magnalia Christi Americana, 1-2
Making of a Counter Culture, 83
Man
   Behaviorist View, 99-100
   Creature, 48
   Fallen, 50-51
   Image of God, 19, 41-42, 47-49
   Marxist View, 91-92, 146-47
   Redeemed, 51
Manicheanism, 116
Marxism, 2, 35, 90-92, 146-47
   Darwinism, 2, 82, 146-47
   Feminism, 96
   Liberation Theology, 92-93
   University, 28, 90

Masonry, 124
Masters of the Universe, 123
Materialism, 55, 72, 82
Mather, Cotton, 1
Maya, 109
Meaning, 62-63, 73
Medieval period, 133
Megatrends, 87
Mein Kampf, 36
"A Mighty Fortress is Our Man," 25
Milky Way Galaxy, 74
Mind at the End of His Tether, The, 78, 81, 137
Mind Reading, 124
Miracles, 56, 66
Modern Language Association, 94
Monism, 85, 87, 88
    Occultism, 118-19, 146
    See also Naturalism; Pantheism
Monist League, 146
Montesquieu, Baron de, 134
Mormonism, 68, 104, 105, 108
Moslems, 68
Multiculturalism, 140, 141
Multiversity, 33
"My Sweet Lord," 85

National Socialist Teachers' League, 36
Naturalism, 35, 40, 53-59, 72, 73, 77, 82
    Behaviorism, 99, 101
    Definition, 54
    Irrationalism, 83
    See also Humanism; Secularism
Nazism, 2, 36, 82, 135, 137, 147
Neutrality
    Myth, 23-25, 32, 39-40, 147-48
    See also Epistemology; Presupposition; Worldview
New Age Humanism, 66, 87-89, 105, 108, 109, 124
New Age Politics, 87
New Humanism, 97-98
New Political Science, 90
Newton, Isaac, 134
New World Translation, 104
New York Times, 58

Nicaraguan Resistance, 28
Night Stalker Murders, 115
Nightmare on Elm Street, 129
The Nightmare Years, 36
Northwestern University, 28

Occult, 88, 115-29
    Biblical View, 124-25
    Flim-Flam, 125
    See also Satanism; Irrationalism; New Age Humanism
Omen, The, 117
Openness, 67
Operant Conditioning, 99
Origin of Species, The (1859), 73, 82, 146
    See also Darwin, Charles; Darwinism; Evolution
Orthopraxy, 139
Other-worldliness, 120
Ouija Board, 121, 122-23, 124
Outline of History, The, 78, 81, 137
Oxford Socratic Club, 69

Paganism, 120-21
Palm Reading, 124
Pantheism, 86
    See also Monism
Pascal's Wager, 76
Pearl of Great Price, 104
Pedophilia, 58
Perspectives, 30-31
Pessimism, 78-79, 81
Pharisees, 11
Philistinism, 97
Pioneer, 74
Planet of the Apes, 55
Pluralism, 67
Political correctness, 140
"Pop" Occultism, 121-23
Postmodernism, 131-44
Positivism, 134
Premodernism, 132-33
Presupposition, 30-32, 143, 145-46
    Definition, 30
    Inescapable, 32
    See also Worldview
Prisoners of War (POWs), 38-39

SUBJECT INDEX

Privatized Christianity, 24, 29, 37
Psychic Healing, 124, 126
Psychological Seduction, 111
Psychology, 98-100
Public Education, 21, 37

Radicalization, 38-39
Rapture, 112
Rationalism, 72
  Irrational, 83
  Occult, 119, 121
  See also Irrationalism
Rationality, 68-70
  Definition, 68
Rationalism-Irrationalism Alliance, 73, 75, 83
Reason, 70-71, 81, 135
  Definition, 13
  See also Rationality; Rationalism; Irrationalism
Rebellion Against God, 51, 49
Redemption, 51
Reduction of Christianity, 118-19
Reformation, the, 1-2, 132
Reincarnation, 66, 86-87
Relativism, 17, 34, 57, 59-61, 67, 131-32, 140
Religion
  Inescapable, 13-14, 19, 20, 21, 22-23, 24, 65-66
  Definition, 23
Religion and Politics, 37
Renaissance, the, 132
Resurrection, 16, 17, 34
Revelation, 49-50, 54, 72, 135
Rise and Fall of the Third Reich, 36
Roe v. Wade (1973), 60
Rosemary's Baby, 117

Sadducees, 11
Salem's Lot, 128
Salvation
  Cults, 109
Santa Claus, 75
Satan
  Biblical View, 118
  Popular Images, 117-18

Satanism, 21, 115-16, 124
Science and Health with Key to the Scriptures, 104-5
Scientism, 41, 81
Scientology, 105
Screwtape Letters, 117
Seances, 124
Secular Humanism, 134-35
Secularism, 24
  Definition, 55
Secularization, 65
Separation of Church and State, 29
Sexual Equality, 96
Shape of Things to Come, The, 137
She-Ra, Princess of Power, 123
The Shining, 128
Sin, 15, 82
  Effects, 50-51
Sixties
  Eastern Religion, 88
  University, 89-90
Skepticism, 11, 13-16, 148
  Healthy, 18
  Naturalism, 56
Slavery, 37, 135
Smith, Adam, 134
Smorgasbord Mentality, 66-67
Snow White, 117
Sociobiology, 100
Son of Sam killings, 116
Sorcery, 124
Space Exploration, 74-77
Speaking, 163
Special Revelation, 50
Spiritualism, 66, 124
Spirituality
  Definition, 19-20
Spiritual Counterfeits, 103-13
Spiritual Counterfeits Project, 88
Spiritual Preparedness, 19-22
Spiritual Substitutes, 21
Star Wars, 85
Statism, 25, 40, 41-43, 48-49, 58-59
  Marxism, 82, 146-47
Stoics, 13
Subjectivism, 83
Suicide, 68-70

Summer Solstice Party, 95
Supreme Court, 61
"Sweetness and Light," 98

Tarot Cards, 124
Technology, 37, 57, 81, 82
Tender Mercies, 31
Tennessee Tech, 28
Term Papers
   See Writing
Tests
   See Exams
Teutons, 121
Theosophy, 105
Thriller, 128
Time Management
   See Scheduling
Time, 82
The Time Machine, 78, 81
Toleration, 58, 67
Tower of Babel, 142-43
Transcendence, 46
   Definition, 15
   Immanence, 46
Transcendental Meditation, 85, 88
Transmigration, 87
Trinity, 46, 105-6
Truth, 71
Tooth Fairy, 75
The Turning Point, 87

Unbelief
   Domino Effect, 52-61
   Hostility to God, 17
Unidentified Flying Objects (UFOs), 124
Unification Church, 104, 108, 109
United Nations Declaration of Human
   Rights (1948), 59
Unity, 105, 108

University
   Decline, 18-19, 42
   Hostility to Christianity, 8, 17, 27, 33
   Marxism, 90
   "Openness," 18, 27-28, 39, 67
   Rebellion, 83, 89-90
   Unity of Knowledge, 33
University of Chicago, 97
Unknown God, 13, 16
Utopia, 37

Vietnam War, 138
Viking, 74
Voyager, 74

War of the Worlds, x, 78, 81
Watchtower, 104
Way International, 105, 108
White Album, 85
William Paterson College, 94
Witchcraft, 115, 120-21, 124, 125
Wizard of Oz, 117
World War I, 82, 135, 137
World War II, 36, 135, 137
Worldview, 27-38
   Christian, 8-10, 45-61
   Coherent, 34-35
   Conflict, 17-19, 25, 35-37
   Definition, 8, 29-30
   Evidence, 34-35
   Exclusive, 35-37
   Humanistic, 2-3
   Inescapable, 13, 24
   Jigsaw, 29
   Presuppositions, 30-33
   Regeneration, xii, 16
   Reason, 13
   Transformational, 37-38
   Unified, 33-34
Worldwide Church of God, 107-8

SCRIPTURE INDEX

Genesis
1:1	33, 106
1:1-2	85
1:31	50
2:15-17	124
3:5	86, 124
3:14-24	124
3:18	50
18:25	106

Exodus
3:13-14	106
7:8-13	113
15:11	47
22:18	124

Leviticus
19:26	125
19:31	124
20:6	124

Deuteronomy
13:1-3	124
18:10	124
18:11	124
18:20-22	124
29:29	47, 125
32:4	47
32:39	106

Judges
9:15	43

1 Samuel
8	43
15:23	125

1 Samuel
28:3-19	124

Job
1:6-22	118
33:4	106

Psalms
8:5	19
19:1-2	49
23	106
27:1	106
47	106
51:4	15
96:13	106
100:3	106
106:21	106
139:7-10	78

Isaiah
6:5	47
22:13	57
40:11	106
40:28	106
41:4	106
43:3	106
43:10	106
43:11	106
44:6	106
44:6-8	106
44:8	86
45:21-23	106
47:9-12	125
47:13	124
48:12	106
60:20	106

WAR OF THE WORLDVIEWS

Jeremiah
8:17	124
10:2	124
10:10	106

Ezekiel
21:21	124

Daniel
2	113

Joel
3:12	106

Matthew
2:1-6	106
2:2	107
2:11	107
4:8-11	113
7:15	113
7:15-23	113
12:30	23
22:33	11
22:34-35	11
22:46	11
24:5	113
24:11	113
26:3-5	11
28:9	107
28:13	34

Mark
3:27	118

Luke
10:18	118
11:20	118
22:21-23	124

John
1:1	106
1:1-3	106
1:9	106
1:14	106
3:19-20	17
4:42	106
8:12	106

John
8:24	106
8:58	106
10:11	106
13:19	106
14:6	67
14:30	118
16:11	118
18:5	106
18:36	120
19:15	113
19:21	106
20:28	107
20:29	107

Acts
4:10-12	106
5:36-37	113
10:25-26	107
12:20-23	113
14:11-15	107
15:29	125
17:1-9	113
17:7	36
17:16	13
17:17	13
17:18	13
17:22-33	13-17
17:22	13
17:23	13
17:24	14
17:25	14
17:26	14
17:29	17
17:30	15, 17
17:31	15, 16
17:32	16

Romans
1-2	51
1:18	15, 49
1:20	49
1:21	49
1:23	49
1:24-32	49
8:4-8	20
14:10-12	106
16:20	118

SCRIPTURE INDEX

1 Corinthians
2:12-16	20
10:3	65
10:6-9	125
15:32	57

2 Corinthians
5:10	106
10:3-5	9
11:14	113

Galatians
1:6	103
1:6-8	109
1:6-10	113
4:8	113
5:20	125

Ephesians
5:22-33	96

Colossians
1:12-17	106
1:13	118
2:8	128
2:15	118

1 Timothy
4:3	113
6:13-16	106

2 Timothy
4:1	106
6:21	16

Hebrews
1:3	52
1:8-12	106
11:3	85
13:20	106

James
4:7	118

1 Peter
3:15	10
5:4	106

1 John
2:19	113
3:8	118
4:1	20, 124
4:1-3	113
4:14	106
5:18	118

Revelation
1:17	106
2:8	106
2:14	125
9:21	125
12:7FF	118
12:9	118
13:11-18	113
14:1	113
19:10	107
22:9	106
22:13	106

About American Vision
Dedicated to Serving Your Educational Needs

American Vision is a non-profit, Christian educational organization which provides materials to help Christians develop a biblical worldview. The Bible tells us: "All Scripture is given by inspiration of God and is profitable for doctrine, for reproof, for correction, for instruction in righteousness; that the man of God may be equipped for every good work" (2 Timothy 3:16-17). Our mission is to clearly demonstrate how biblical principles apply to every area of life, including family, church, education, economics, the arts, law, medicine, journalism, business, and civil government.

American Vision is dedicated to the goal of helping Christians think biblically, because through individual lives transformed by the power of Jesus Christ, society will also be changed to reflect Christ's lordship over all of life. To this end American Vision produces the highest quality educational material: books, audio and video tapes, newsletters and magazines. *Biblical Worldview* is American Vision's monthly publication, edited by Gary DeMar, and is offered on a donation basis.

American Vision also arranges radio debates, television interviews, lectures, and special conferences. The goal before us is to spread the message of Christ's victorious reign. You can participate in the work of American Vision by subscribing to *Biblical Worldview*, reading our other material, and supporting us through your prayers and tax-deductible contributions. Join with us as we work to spread the good news that Jesus Christ is Savior and Lord.

For Further Information write to

American Vision
10 Perimeter Way, B-175
Atlanta, GA 30339
404-988-0555